TWENTY DINNERS

TWENTY DINNERS

ITHAI SCHORI & CHRIS TAYLOR

WITH RACHEL HOLTZMAN

PHOTOGRAPHS BY NICOLE FRANZEN

CLARKSON POTTER/PUBLISHERS
NEW YORK

Copyright © 2015 by Ithai Schori and Chris Taylor
Photographs copyright © 2015 by Nicole Franzen

All rights reserved.
Published in the United States by Clarkson Potter/Publishers, an imprint of the Crown Publishing Group, a division of Random House LLC, a Penguin Random House Company, New York.
www.crownpublishing.com
www.clarksonpotter.com

CLARKSON POTTER is a trademark and POTTER with colophon is a registered trademark of Random House LLC.

Library of Congress Cataloging-in-Publication Data
Schori, Ithai.
  Twenty dinners / Chris Taylor and Ithai Schori; with Rachel Holtzman.—First edition.
     pages cm
1. Dinners and dining. 2. Entertaining.
3. Menus. I. Taylor, Chris (Musician)
II. Holtzman, Rachel. III. Title.
  TX731.S335 2014
  641.5'4—dc23

2014036811

ISBN 978-0-385-34528-6
eBook ISBN 978-0-385-34529-3

Printed in China

Design by Stephanie Huntwork
Jacket photographs by Nicole Franzen

10 9 8 7 6 5 4 3 2 1

First Edition

CHRIS

This book is dedicated to my friends who, many times, have waited for hours for me to finish dinner. But most of all, I dedicate my work to my mother, who passed along her love and knowledge of cooking to a young, hungry kid and showed me how fun and rewarding it is to feed your friends and family.

ITHAI

To my family, friends, and anyone I ever have or will share a meal with. Meet you there.

CONTENTS

INTRODUCTION

This book started when Ithai showed up at a barbecue in Chris's backyard and jumped in to help cook. We'd met before through mutual friends, but it was once we got into the kitchen together that things clicked. We shared a passion for making good food happen and feeding our friends, but in a laid-back way. After that night, if there was a party we went to, we'd end up being the guys in the kitchen. We'd get in there with no agenda—we cooked with whatever was handy and riffed off each other's ideas. We'd experiment with new flavor combinations or try out something we'd read in a book, always wanting to learn more.

The kitchen was just where we'd rather be, but it always turned out that was where the real gathering was anyway. Our friends weren't sitting around the table waiting for food—they were helping prep or clean or just hanging out with us. There was no "Dinner will be served at eight o'clock." It was more like "Okay, open another bottle of wine because we forgot to put the burgers on." It was delicious, fun, simple, and it couldn't have been more relaxing.

These days, Chris spends most of his time on tour with his band, but whenever he comes back, one of the first things that happens is we start up the grill—no matter what time of year—and get all our friends together. It's a great excuse to cook up a big cut of meat and reconnect. Aside from turning out some tasty things for dinner, we really like how happy our food makes people—especially when we put out great classic dishes or childhood favorites like rib eye steaks or roast chicken but do them up with a little something extra, like potatoes roasted with duck fat or kale salad with brown-butter pine nuts.

Every step of the way, our friends have come along for the ride, which is what makes every meal that much more special. They show up at our impromptu dinners, let us take over their kitchens, are eager recipe testers, and contribute to our gatherings plenty of booze, records, firewood, desserts, and good conversation. More than the food, that's what getting together is all about. So many of us have moved away from the families we grew up with. But it's our friends who become a family of a different kind. Bringing everyone together to share a meal, stories, laugh, complain about work or the subway, or just generally put folks' day behind them is what we consider a truly family affair.

That's why we wrote this book. It's a cookbook, yes, of twenty big dinners' worth of recipes, our favorite techniques, and points of inspiration, but it's really about giving you the ideas and tools to make these kinds of gatherings happen for you and your friends.

We can't tell you how many times we've been cooking and someone has said, "I could never do that." Or how many times one of us has asked a friend to do some cutting, cleaning, or check on what's happening on the stove and gotten a totally freaked-out look in response. Simple things like cutting up an onion or blanching some green beans seemed intimidating. Or worse, we'd watch friends run back and forth between a cookbook and the stove, too stressed by a recipe to enjoy what they were doing or spend time with the people around them.

So we set out to change that.

Instead of taking over the kitchen to make dinner, we invite everyone to help. We don't want to cook *for* our friends—we want to cook *with* them. We want to get our friends to drop all the hang-ups they have about making something good to eat. And to do that we would show them what we've both learned through a lot of cooking: That great meals happen when you get rid of the idea that they have to come from a fancy chef or restaurant or strict recipe. That cooking can be easy and easygoing. That *blanching* is really just a fancy word for "cook for a few seconds in salted, boiling water." That in the time it takes to peel the plastic off the top of a tub of dip, they could grill some zucchini, hit it with a little olive oil and salt, and serve that instead. Or poach an egg. Or make a vinaigrette for a simple salad. That simplicity is what's impressive, not flipping out over ridiculously complicated dishes. That no one said dinner has to start and end at the table (or even make it to the table). That another beer / cocktail / bottle of wine goes a long way in erasing any culinary miscalculations. And most important, at the end of the day, that it's just making something to eat.

So how do you cook great food and have a good time doing it? For us, it starts with nailing the basics—learning how to prepare ingredients, understanding how they taste, and thinking about how each ingredient will ultimately turn into something you want to eat. All you need are a few techniques in your repertoire, some high-quality ingredients in your pantry, and maybe a few friends to help shuck, peel, dice, or babysit the action on the stove. From there, it's really just about dancing a little more in the kitchen.

Look, we're not chefs. We don't run restaurants and we're not in a professional kitchen working dinner service every night. We do all this stuff at home, which is why we believe that you can do the same. Neither of us pretends to have some golden key to culinary excellence, but what we do have is experience. We've been able to learn from our mistakes, and now we're passing that on so you don't have to get there the hard way. We've also picked up really great ways to get the most out of what we're cooking, and the simplest, most straightforward methods to do it. But our goal isn't only to get you cooking the perfect steak (which you will) or knowing how to make your own pickled vegetables (yes, even that)—we're going to help you trust your own instincts so you can just get in the kitchen and jam.

CHRIS'S STORY

I swear, my mom could *smell* when I was cutting an onion wrong. I first learned about cooking by hanging out in the kitchen with her, an amazing cook who learned from her mom.

No matter how high the tree I had climbed at the park or how much I might have wanted to stay out with friends, I always came home in time for dinner. I was always there to help my mom cook—preparing vegetables and meat by her specific requests. When I did it wrong, she'd *always* notice and would patiently ask me to do it again, telling me why we were cutting things up a certain way and how different cuts cooked at different rates, which is why you wanted everything to be the same size. No kid likes to be corrected, but with Mom in the kitchen, it never felt like I had to follow too many rules; it felt like learning how to do it right. Maybe not the first time, but sometimes by my second try—which is how it works when learning how to cook. She and I would also talk about the differences among all kinds of oils, vinegars, and salts and why we would use certain ingredients at certain times and their role in building the flavor of a dish. Over time, I learned how all these things tasted and how to use them when I was cooking.

Like any person really trying to improve at something, I would lie awake in bed, digesting all that I learned and tried, consumed with how I would change my approach the next time we cooked. One of the first more-involved dishes I was trusted to make on my own was chili when I was around ten years old. I was pretty decent at following recipes, but I wanted to elaborate. Because I loved spicy food, I found everything spicy in the cupboard and added at will: cayenne pepper, chili powder, crushed red pepper, hot sauce, every bottle that had a drawing of flames. You can probably guess what happened—the chili was inedibly spicy. I learned that making food too spicy meant flavor took a backseat to heat. So the next time I made chili, I took note of each spice I added as I included it. And eventually, the food I cooked got better and better each time I gave it a go.

I've frequently been told that you really understand why people play golf once you play your first "good game," and I believe making food is no different. The first thing you make that you really love to eat—even if it's as simple as a nicely dressed salad or a plate of nachos (which actually was my first "good game" dish at ten years old)—is all it takes to fall in love with cooking. Well, after a few good games, I was hooked. My mom and I would cook together for two whole days when our family hosted Thanksgiving. I'm proud to say that my entire extended family will still attest that the best food on any given holiday was at our house. By the time I was fifteen, I was sometimes given the responsibility of being the sole cook for my family's dinners. As I got a little older, I translated the same passion into learning in professional kitchens and, most of all, hosting dinner parties for my friends.

These days, I spend most of my time on the road playing music, and cooking isn't something I can do as often as I like, which is to say as often as humanly possible. Finding something decent to eat in the first place can be a challenge. When I wake up in a new town every morning, walking out of the bus bleary-eyed and not sure what street I'm on or even where the venue or my bandmates are, food isn't usually my first priority of the day—it's finding a clean shower, for starters. But the one thing I miss the most while I'm away, more than any other comfort of home, is having friends over to eat. Going grocery shopping. And when I get back, I hit the farmers' market, get inspired about what's in season, and that's when I know I've truly arrived home. I know it may sound silly to be excited about grocery shopping, but for me it's the beginning of the creative process I love so much. You can express a lot in the food you are cooking, whether that be to provide comfort or excitement. Sometimes it's fun to make an evening into more of a dinner party "event," or sometimes you just need to eat—fun in its own right since you need to work within culinary limits, yet still satisfy. It also reminds me of how much my mom loved cooking for us. I know that's why I find it so valuable to eat delicious food with close friends and family. I think music and cooking are a lot alike in that way for me— both tend to mean the most when shared. I enjoy every minute of taking way too long to get everything done because it just means everyone gets to hang out longer. There's often no rush for me to get dinner ready because it's not merely about the food we're going to eat but also about the time spent making it in good company, listening to records, drinking some wine, and catching up on each other's lives between bites. Few things in life are as satisfying and simple.

ITHAI'S STORY

Oh man, I used to make some of the worst food when I was a kid. My parents would go out for the night and I would try to cook something for my brother and me. An ambitious kid in a kitchen is not a pretty sight, and there were definitely nights when my brother went to sleep hungry. I think he still has nightmares from the time I tried to make a stir-fry. I thought all there was to it was grabbing everything in the fridge, stirring it together, and throwing some soy sauce on it. I was wrong. Really, really wrong. But over time, I got better.

My grandfather used to say, "There are two kinds of people in this world: those who eat to live and those who live to eat." It's fair to say I have always been the latter—and it's what first drew me to cooking. I realized quickly that if you make something good, you get to eat it, too. And being in the kitchen is pretty awesome. Ever since those terrible stir-fry dinners, I've loved getting lost in the rhythm of the kitchen. To this day, it's my version of running around in the mud—messy and satisfying. It's a place where I can just grab a beer, listen to a good album, and allow whatever's going on around me to recede.

For a couple of years, I was lucky enough to work professionally in some really good kitchens, surrounded by amazing cooks and chefs. One night, after service, we were all hanging out at the restaurant's bar when our chef, Peter Serpico, told us to go downstairs and grab some of the extra prime rib that was in the walk-in. But instead of doing some complex prep to it for guests the next day, we made steak and eggs for ourselves while we drank beers until four in the morning. It was a cool reminder not to take food too seriously: Here we were, working in one of the country's top kitchens, getting more excited about glorified diner food than some crazy reduction. It also made me realize how incredible it was to cook alongside and learn from guys like Serpico and Sean Grey, two of the best cooks in the city, and how easy it felt to come together at the table when the pressure of service was off.

It was a pretty rough wake-up call when I left the professional cook route and started making food in my apartment again. I went from a playground stocked with an endless supply of tools and ingredients to what felt like cooking with an Easy-Bake oven. After spending sixteen hours a day nursing dishes from start to finish, using truly great ingredients, I was getting home after sixteen hours on a photo shoot and just needing something to eat.

The funny thing, though, is that going back to being a home cook forced me to become a better cook. I began to simplify things as much as possible, focusing more on technique and finding good ingredients that never required much messing with anyway. When you're trained to make everything you need from scratch instead of buying it, but then find yourself without a team of cooks surrounding you, you learn to simplify what you *think* you need. And the limited space and equipment forced me to become more efficient. I had two knives and a cast-iron pan, and it worked.

I had the same epiphany about simplicity when we started writing this book. The more I tried to shove recipes into rigid times, measurements, and temperatures, the worse the food was. I've always just felt my way through cooking, going by intuition instead of always looking at a clock or thermometer. The recipes in this book are my way of getting back to the kind of cooking I fell in love with all over again after leaving the restaurant world. It's the kind of food that doesn't need strict rules and guidelines to be good. It's the opposite—it gets better with a little more love and a little more dancing.

I also realized how much more I'd rather cook with people than for them, especially if someone's asked me to teach them how to cook. It's the best, most enjoyable way to make good food and learn a few things in the process. Instead of getting wrapped up in a recipe or stuck on learning "perfect" technique, it's a chance to kick back and actually hang out. And the food is so much better that way, too. There's nothing wrong with aspiring to re-create restaurant food at home. But what people don't realize is that when making those kinds of dishes, you're doing the work of ten people. Whole teams of professional cooks dedicate their lives to making that kind of food. It's so much more enjoyable when we stop trying to cook like the people who are getting paid to do it all day, every day. And I've found that the home-cooked meal that people often long for is rarely about the actual dish. It's about the people and the time we get to spend together.

ABOUT THIS BOOK AND THE RECIPES

We want you to tear this book apart—write in the margins, cross things out, change things around. There's no way we could possibly know what kind of ingredients you like or how you'll season them or who you're going to be eating them with. These twenty dinners' worth of recipes, from a simple night in to an elaborate gathering for friends, are things that we personally like, but it's cool to tailor a dish or a menu to your taste—take a dish from one menu and serve it with one from another or borrow a component from one dish and put it on another. Whether or not you like fennel, that's your call. And honestly, it'd be crazy to spend all day going to six different places to find celery root; just use parsnip or turnips instead.

While both of us dig into cookbooks for inspiration and reference, we think it's possible to rely on recipes a little too much. Cooking isn't about following directions to the letter; it's about building a foundation of basics and trusting yourself to use them. The key is to understand reasons behind things like getting a good sear on a piece of meat or using a particular flour to pan-fry fish or why some ingredients taste better together than others. Then you're on your way to getting amped, experimenting, and having way more of a good time than you would with your face all up in a book.

Our recipes aren't meant to be mandates as much as guidelines. We'll include specific measurements to give you a place to start, but most of the time we're not big fans of having to portion everything out to the eighth of a teaspoon (except in baking recipes, where precision *is* more important). And beyond a few simple "rules," often there's no one right way to do something—only the way that's right for you.

Really, we're just trying to set you up with the confidence to try new things, to know what you like, and to trust yourself. And if it doesn't come out exactly as you hoped the first time, that's fine. Chances are it didn't for us either. But no worries, it only gets better the more you try—and it just gives you an excuse to have your friends over again.

PLATING
You'll notice that we don't serve all our dishes family-style. That's because when you arrange food in front of guests you're essentially suggesting to them how you want them to eat it. It's a weird thing, but if you put everything in separate piles, most people end up eating each component separately and missing out on how the dishes mix with one another. Here's another way to think about it: You toss a salad before serving it, right? See, you're plating and you didn't even realize it.

You can plate food so that people will taste every flavor and component without even thinking about it. It's nothing fancy or complicated—it's as simple as putting your cauliflower puree underneath your duck breast instead of next to it. That way someone eating the dish will get a little of everything with each bite.

A WORD ON OUR DESSERTS

We're not really dessert guys. When we do want something sweet, it will usually be simple like a bowl of cherries or a scoop of ice cream with some sea salt on top (both of which make appearances in this book). But we recognize the importance—and tastiness—of finishing a meal right, so we called on our friend Lillie O'Brien to be our guest pastry chef for this book.

After leaving Australia for a brief cooking stint in Japan, she found her way to St. John Bread and Wine, one of London's top eateries. Working as a pastry chef, she found a passion for concocting deliciously atypical jams, which ultimately turned into her successful business, London Borough of Jam.

In her baking, Lillie embraces seasonal flavors, pairing the unexpected—peach and fennel blossom, fig and Earl Grey. And her desserts embrace the same simplicity in approach as we strive for with our menus, which is perfect if you've ever been a little bit afraid of baking.

FALL

DINNER 1

Sliced Fluke, Plum, and Cilantro

———

Seared Kale Salad with Brown Butter–Toasted
Pine Nuts and Smoked Bacon

———

Roast Chicken

———

Morel and Shiitake Mushroom Risotto

———

Maple Panna Cotta with Candied Almonds
and Buttered Bread Crumbs

WHAT TO DRINK

A dry, light white, such as Grüner Veltliner,
or a very light red, such as an Old Vine Cru Beaujolais

SLICED FLUKE, PLUM,
AND CILANTRO

SERVES 4 TO 6

We're not usually into fruit with seafood, or most savory things, for that matter. But here the plum gives you a little tartness, like you would get with a lemon, just with a bit more sweetness.

All you have to keep in mind for making *crudo* (Italian for "raw") is finding the freshest fish possible. You should feel really good about the fish you buy to eat raw.

1 8-ounce fluke fillet or another white-fleshed fish like sea bass

1 purple plum, pitted and sliced paper thin

Fresh cilantro leaves

Good-quality extra-virgin olive oil, for finishing

Fleur de sel or other flaky salt

Look closely at your fish; there will probably be a few white lines running through the fillet. This is the sinew. Slice the fish into clean, thin slices about ¼ inch thick, cutting perpendicular to the lines of sinew.

Top each slice with a sliver of plum, a cilantro leaf, a bit of oil, and fleur de sel. It's that easy.

SEARED KALE SALAD
WITH BROWN BUTTER–TOASTED PINE NUTS AND SMOKED BACON

SERVES 4 TO 6

This salad is the answer to people who think they don't like leafy greens. Good kale has a deep, almost meaty flavor. Searing it and mixing it with brown-butter-drenched pine nuts, sweet raisins, and salty Parmesan cheese is a no-fail treatment. Most other hearty greens like beet greens, dandelion greens, or radish tops would also be good in this dish.

---

2 large bunches of kale, thick stems removed, washed and dried (see page 255)

Olive oil

Salt and freshly ground black pepper

1 shallot, finely diced

¼ cup dry white wine (something you'd be okay drinking)

4 strips thick-cut smoky bacon, cut into bite-size pieces

Handful of raisins, preferably golden

Handful of pine nuts, toasted (see page 255)

1 lemon

Parmesan cheese, broken by hand into small bite-friendly chunks

Roughly chop or tear the kale into large but manageable bite-size pieces.

In a large skillet, add just enough oil to coat the bottom and heat over a high flame until it smokes. Add just enough kale to make one layer. Cook the kale until it is slightly softened and bright green but still crunchy, giving it a toss every couple minutes. Add salt and pepper to taste. Transfer the kale to a large bowl and allow it to cool; it will continue to soften. Cook the rest of the kale in batches, wiping out your skillet after each batch.

Coat the skillet with oil. Set it over low heat and add the shallot. Sauté until translucent, about 5 minutes. Season with a pinch of salt, then pour in the wine and ¼ cup water. Bring to a boil and then immediately turn the heat down to a slow simmer. Let the liquid reduce until it has almost but not quite evaporated, about 10 minutes. Pour the contents of the skillet over the cooked kale and allow it to cool.

Return the cooled skillet over low heat and add the bacon. Slowly render the fat until the bacon is crispy. Transfer the bacon to a paper-towel-lined dish to drain. Add to the kale.

Top the kale with the raisins and nuts. Squeeze the lemon over the top and add the Parmesan to taste. Toss all to combine and serve.

ROAST CHICKEN

SERVES 4

Roast chicken is where we begin for a couple of reasons. First, it's a delicious staple that everyone loves, especially when care is taken to do it nicely. Second, learning how to make the perfect roast chicken is a great way to understand how to roast meat in general. Our method calls for browning it first in a hot cast-iron skillet and then roasting it gently to keep the meat tender. And with chicken, the stakes are a little lower than learning how to cook a more expensive cut of meat. For about ten bucks, you can get the happiest, free-roaming chicken on the planet and feed four people.

---

1 chicken (about 3 pounds)

4 tablespoons (½ stick) unsalted butter

Salt

3 sprigs fresh rosemary

3 sprigs fresh thyme

2 sprigs fresh sage

5 garlic cloves, smashed

1½ lemons, cut into wedges

Coarse salt and freshly ground black pepper

Thirty minutes before cooking the chicken, take it out of the fridge and pat dry with a paper towel.

Preheat the oven to 325°F.

Heat a large cast-iron skillet over a medium flame and add the butter. It should be enough to coat the bottom of your skillet. Once the butter starts to foam, season the bird with salt, then place it in the skillet (any side down is fine) and allow to brown, 6 to 8 minutes.

Once the first side has a nice golden crust, flip the chicken and repeat the browning process on the remaining three sides. To avoid getting splattered with hot butter and rendered chicken fat, tip the skillet away from you when flipping the chicken. Sticking a long pair of tongs into the cavity of the bird is a good way to handle the flipping.

When the entire chicken is browned, take it off the heat and drop the rosemary, thyme, sage, and garlic into the cavity. Keep the chicken in he skillet or, ideally, transfer to a rack set on top of a rimmed baking sheet. Using the already-hot skillet can cook the bird unevenly on one side. Also, a rack allows hot air to circulate all the way around the bird. Either way, put the chicken in the oven.

Roast the bird until a cake tester feels hot to the touch (see page 252) or the chicken has reached an internal temperature of 145°F, about 1 hour, or roughly 20 minutes per pound.

Once the bird is cooked, remove it from the oven and let it rest for 10 minutes on a rack, loosely covered with foil. Squeeze lemon juice over the top and finish it with coarse salt and pepper.

MOREL AND SHIITAKE MUSHROOM RISOTTO

SERVES 4 TO 6

Italians might take issue with us for saying so, but risotto is really just a porridge with a little more stirring, so don't sweat the myth that it's hard to make. And when you add other ingredients to it like mushrooms, the rice soaks up all that flavor. So it's not just rice and mushrooms, it's rice *with* mushrooms. And when you add butter and cheese . . . definitely.

2 tablespoons unsalted butter

1 large shallot, finely diced

4 cups chicken stock

1 large garlic clove, minced

1 cup Arborio rice

½ cup dry white wine

6 fresh morel mushrooms, cleaned, stemmed, small ones halved and large ones quartered

6 fresh shiitake mushrooms, cleaned, stemmed, and sliced

Salt and freshly ground black pepper

½ cup grated Parmesan cheese

Zest of 2 lemons

½ bunch of fresh parsley, roughly chopped

In a medium saucepan over medium heat, melt 1 tablespoon of the butter. Add the shallot to the pan and let it sweat. In another small saucepan over medium-high heat, warm your chicken stock.

Once the shallot has become translucent, after about 5 minutes, add your garlic and sweat for another minute. Then add your rice to the shallot-garlic mixture and stir until everything is coated with butter.

Now add the wine and stir constantly until it is absorbed. Ladle in the hot stock, 1 cup at a time, stirring after each addition. When the stock is nearly evaporated, add more. When you are about halfway through the stock, add the mushrooms. Continue adding stock and stirring until your rice is tender and looks "plump," about 15 minutes total. Taste for doneness and season with salt and pepper. Keep in mind that the Parmesan will add saltiness, too. Remove the pan from the heat.

Stir in the remaining tablespoon of butter, then the Parmesan. Allow your risotto to rest for 2 to 3 minutes at the back of your stovetop, covered. (Letting risotto rest is an underrated step. These couple of minutes allow the rice to fully absorb its liquid and cook through properly.) Add the lemon zest and parsley. Check for seasoning and add more salt and pepper if desired. Serve!

MAPLE PANNA COTTA
WITH CANDIED ALMONDS AND BUTTERED BREAD CRUMBS
SERVES 4 TO 6

Most panna cottas are set with so much gelatin that they look and feel like jiggly bricks. We love a creamier style that melts when you bite it, so we've kept the consistency loose and the presentation more free form. And by adding buttery brioche crumbs, candied almonds, some mint, and smoky sea salt, we've taken this too-often bland dessert to a much happier place.

---

1 cup whole milk

2 gelatin sheets

1 cup heavy cream

¼ cup plus ½ tablespoon pure maple syrup

1 whole vanilla bean, split lengthwise

¼ teaspoon kosher salt

1 generous tablespoon unsalted butter

⅓ cup brioche bread crumbs, ground to roughly the size of panko crumbs

½ cup almonds, roughly chopped

Fresh mint leaves

Smoked coarse sea salt

In a large saucepan over medium heat, combine the milk, heavy cream, and ¼ cup maple syrup and bring to a low simmer. Reduce the heat so the milk is steaming, not bubbling. Scrape the vanilla pod's seeds into the milk, whisk to combine, and add the pod. Steep the pod until it has softened and wilted. Remove the pot from the heat and retrieve the pod.

Place the gelatin sheets in a small bowl of cold water for 5 to 7 minutes until softened while the vanilla bean is steeping. Remove the sheets and squeeze them to remove excess water, then add them to the vanilla-infused cream mixture while it's still hot. Whisk to completely dissolve the gelatin.

Stir in the kosher salt and pour the mixture into a heavy baking dish. Let cool to room temperature, cover with plastic wrap, and refrigerate for 6 hours or overnight until fully set.

Over medium heat in a medium saucepan, melt the butter and let it come to a nutty brown color. Toast the bread crumbs in the butter until lightly golden. Remove and drain on a paper-towel-lined plate.

In a small saucepan over medium-high heat, combine the remaining ½ tablespoon maple syrup and the almonds and toss to candy, 1 to 2 minutes or until the syrup moves easily in the pan. Remove from the heat and evenly spread the nuts on a piece of parchment to cool completely.

To serve, put a slice of panna cotta onto each plate and sprinkle with the almonds, bread crumbs, and mint. Finish each dish with a pinch of sea salt.

DINNER 2

Pan-Roasted Duck Breast

Cauliflower Puree

Braised Cipollini Onions

Shaved Brussels Sprouts

Spiced Red Wine–Poached Pears

WHAT TO DRINK

Spiked Apple Crisp

Dry cider (ciders from Normandy or the Basque country
are special and delicious) or a light red Burgundy

SPIKED APPLE CRISP

MAKES 10 TO 12 COCKTAILS

Try this without alcohol for a warm kid-friendly drink or substitute other spirits when adults imbibe, like dark rum, bourbon, or rye. You can add or subtract ingredients here. Sometimes I use cardamom, or when it's made with rum, I add more ginger. —*Nino*

½ gallon fresh, unfiltered apple cider

Zest of 1 orange

Zest of 1 lemon

5 or 6 cloves

4 or 5 allspice berries

1 teaspoon freshly grated nutmeg

¼ cup light brown sugar, packed

4 cinnamon sticks

1 or 2 star anise pods

2 to 3 ½-inch slices of peeled fresh ginger

10 to 24 ounces Calvados brandy, to your preference

Add the cider, orange zest, lemon zest, cloves, allspice berries, nutmeg, sugar, cinnamon sticks, star anise, and ginger to a large pot. Cover, bring to a simmer, and let warm for 20 minutes. Using a ladle and fine-mesh sieve, strain the hot cider into mugs. Add to this 1 or 2 ounces Calvados brandy. Sip till cured of all that ails you.

Shake all ingredients except the celery with ice and strain into a glass filled with ice. Garnish with the celery.

PAN-ROASTED DUCK BREAST

SERVES 4

Some people get stressed out when it comes to cooking duck because they think it's going to be complicated. But the whole reason duck is one of our favorite things to make is because it's unbelievably simple. All you have to do to get perfectly crispy skin and juicy, tender meat is slowly render out the fat. From there, just finish it with a little butter and you have a quintessential fall meat that's made for earthy, sweet vegetables like cauliflower and braised cipollini onions.

---

4 small Muscovy or 2 large Magret duck breasts

Salt

Freshly ground black pepper

1 generous tablespoon unsalted butter

1 to 2 garlic cloves, smashed

2 sprigs fresh thyme

To help the duck fat render, gently run the length of your knife across the fatty side of the breast. Move in diagonal lines, leaving about ¼ inch between them, and slicing down to just before where the skin meets the flesh. Turn the breast 90 degrees and repeat—you should have what looks like a little diamond pattern. Season the skin side with salt.

Situate your duck breasts skin side down in a cold cast-iron skillet, no oil necessary. Season the meat with salt and pepper and put the pan over low heat. As the duck releases its fat, periodically remove it from the skillet with a large spoon, add it to a small glass or mason jar, and save it. You'll want to store it in your fridge or freezer for making Slow-Roasted Duck Fat Potatoes (page 79). Be careful not to let the duck contract too much as the heat builds; if it starts to buckle, hold it firmly to the bottom of the skillet with a spoon or your fingers.

Continue letting the breast gently cook, removing the fat, until the skin is crispy and brown. Depending on how much duck you have, this could take 6 minutes, or it could take 15. Use your cake tester to make sure you're at rare—it should feel just warm, not hot. Flip and sear the meat side for just enough time to lightly brown. (You'll be putting them back into the skillet one more time at the very end.) Once done, remove the breasts from the skillet to a cooling rack. Let them rest skin side up for about half the time it took you to cook them. Pour the remaining fat into your jar.

To finish the duck, wipe out the skillet and warm it over medium-high heat. Add the butter to the skillet along with the garlic and thyme. Let the butter get foamy, then add the duck, skin side up. Baste with about 10 good spoonfuls of melted butter, then set the breasts back on the cooling rack and allow them to rest for 1 or 2 minutes more. Slice the duck into ¼-inch slices across the short side; this cuts against the meat's grain.

CAULIFLOWER PUREE

SERVES 6 TO 8

One of our favorite ways to cook vegetables is to simmer them until tender and then let the food processor or blender have at them until they are a smooth puree. The flavor is pure and the texture is luxurious. You can use this method for just about any hearty vegetable. You can also use the leftovers as a base for other meals. Cauliflower is nutty and sweet, so try pairing it with pork, which, like duck, lends itself to sweeter things. Thin it out with some stock for a creamy soup, or just eat it with a spoon as a snack on its own.

---

1 head of garlic, top sliced off, exposing the cloves

4 sprigs fresh thyme

6 whole black peppercorns

1 large head of cauliflower, quartered to remove the core and stem, then broken up into 1-inch pieces

4 cups milk

2 cups heavy cream

Kosher salt

NOTE: OTHER PUREE POSSIBILITIES
You can sub in almost any vegetable here—anything mashable, like carrots—and get a great puree. For pairing with duck in particular, try parsnip or celery root. Just use 6 parsnips, roughly chopped, or 1 to 2 celery roots, peeled and cubed.

Make a bouquet garni by putting the garlic, thyme, and peppercorns in a cheesecloth bundle and tying it with string.

Add the cauliflower to a large saucepan and cover with the milk and cream. Throw in the bouquet garni, add a pinch of salt, bring to a boil over medium-high heat, then reduce to a simmer. Gently cook the cauliflower until it yields easily to a fork or cake tester, about 20 minutes.

Strain the mixture, reserving the liquid and discarding the bouquet garni. Add the cauliflower to a food processor or blender and blend until smooth, adding in some of the cooking liquid to adjust the consistency. It should be just thick enough that a spoonful can hold itself upside down for a half second before falling. Season with salt to taste.

BRAISED
CIPOLLINI ONIONS

SERVES 4

Braised cipollini onions make great bed-fellows with most meats, but their cara-melized sweetness tastes delicious with duck in particular. The longer they cook, the better they get, so don't be afraid of put-ting these guys in the oven in the morning and letting them go low and slow all day. If you're pressed for time, you can up the tem-perature to 300°F and compress the cook time to a couple of hours. Or you can do these a day ahead, stash them in the fridge, and heat them up with a little bit of stock.

---

8 cipollini, pearl, or boiling onions

2 cups chicken or vegetable stock, or as needed

Salt and freshly ground black pepper

Preheat the oven to 225°F.

Place the onions in a baking dish large enough so they sit in one layer and add enough stock so the onions are halfway submerged. Season gently with salt and pepper, then cover the pan with foil and put it in the oven.

Bake for 2 hours, then remove the foil so the onions can begin to caramelize. Check on them every hour to flip them over and make sure there's still moisture in the pan. If there's not, add more stock or water. Cook for 4 to 5 hours total, until the onions are deeply golden and very soft.

SHAVED
BRUSSELS SPROUTS

SERVES 4

We recommend using a mandoline to get the Brussels sprouts nice and thin. The effect is like a fall slaw that pairs with meat as well as it stands on its own.

---

10 to 12 large Brussels sprouts

Olive oil

1 handful of nuts, such as almonds, walnuts, cashews, or chestnuts, chopped

Salt

Pure maple syrup to taste

Lemon juice or sherry vinegar (optional)

To prep the Brussels sprouts, remove two or three of the tougher outer leaves, trim off any remnants of the stem, and halve. Using a mandoline or knife, thinly shave the Brussels sprouts.

Get a medium sauté pan nice and hot over medium-high heat and coat the bottom with oil. When the oil shimmers, hit the Brussels sprouts and nuts hard and fast. You only want the vegetables to wilt a little bit so they're still fresh and have a bit of crunch. Add salt and maple syrup to taste, give a quick toss to com-bine, then remove the pan from the heat. Taste again and adjust the seasoning if desired, pos-sibly adding a little lemon juice or sherry vin-egar if you want to add some bright acidity.

SPICED RED WINE–POACHED PEARS

SERVES 6

After a rich, warm meal like duck it's always nice to eat something slightly earthy and sweet like a poached pear. Pears that have been cooked slowly for a long time—especially in spice-infused red wine—are juicy and delicate and all-around underrated. Just be sure to choose pears that are perfectly ripe. If they're overripe they will overcook, underripe and they won't have flavor.

1 lemon

1 orange

6 ripe pears, such as Concorde, Bosc, Anjou, or Bartlett

6¼ cups sugar

1 bottle of red wine, something you'd be okay drinking

3 star anise pods

1 cinnamon stick

Vanilla ice cream, for serving (optional)

Using a vegetable peeler, carefully remove the zests of the lemon and orange and set aside. Peel the pears (be sure to keep the stems of the pears intact).

In a wide, heavy-bottomed saucepan, combine the sugar, wine, star anise, cinnamon, and lemon and orange zests. Bring the mixture to a boil over medium-high heat, then reduce to a gentle simmer.

Carefully place the pears in the poaching liquid. Cover the pot with parchment paper (if you have it; the parchment acts as extra insulation) and a lid, turn off the heat, and allow the pears to steep for approximately 20 minutes. The cooking time will depend on the pear's ripeness, so use 20 minutes as a general gauge, and turn the heat back on for a while if necessary. The pears are ready when you can easily pierce them with a cake tester.

Transfer the pears to a plate and set aside. Raise the heat up to high and reduce the poaching liquid until it thickens to a syrup. Remove from the heat and let cool.

Chill the pears in the syrup overnight and serve either cold or warmed with a scoop of vanilla ice cream, if desired

FOUR SEASONS OF BURRATA TOASTS

Starting a meal with toast doesn't sound like much, but it's amazing how much people love crisp bread topped with something as simple as some good cheese, fresh herbs, and a little salt and pepper. People always appreciate a snack before dinner, and it helps buy you more time in the kitchen if things are taking a little longer than expected.

FALL

POACHED PEARS AND BACON-MAPLE BURRATA TOAST

SERVES 6

2 cups dry white wine (something you'd be okay drinking)

½ cup sugar

1 or 2 whole star anise pods

2 sprigs fresh rosemary

1 bay leaf

4 pears, peeled, cored, and quartered

1½ cups macadamia nuts, toasted (see page 255) and chopped

1 baguette, cut into ¾-inch slices

Extra-virgin olive oil

1 slice bacon

½ cup pure maple syrup

½ pound burrata

A few leaves of fresh mint, finely chopped

Maldon or other flaky salt

Preheat the oven to 400°F.

In a large saucepan, combine 2 cups water with the wine, sugar, star anise, rosemary, and bay leaf. Bring to a simmer over medium-high heat. Add the pears and cook until they are fork-tender or are easily pierced by a cake tester, 7 to 10 minutes. Strain out the pears and cut them into ½-inch cubes.

In a small mixing bowl, combine the pears and toasted macadamia nuts. Set aside.

Make the toast by first brushing the baguette slices with oil, then browning them in the oven to your liking. Set aside.

In a cast-iron skillet or heavy-bottomed sauté pan over low heat, render out the fat from the bacon (see page 256). Once you've gotten a good tablespoon's worth, remove just the bacon—not the fat—and add the maple syrup. Allow it to reduce for a minute, until quite sticky. Now add the pear mixture and cook for a minute more. Remove from the heat. (Snack on the bacon.)

Spoon the pear mixture over the burrata and finish with fresh mint and Maldon salt. Serve with toasted bread.

WINTER

FENNEL AND GRAPEFRUIT BURRATA TOAST

SERVES 6

Supremes of 1 grapefruit, cut in half (see Note)

1 small bulb of fennel, sliced as thinly as possible (a mandoline works well for this), fronds reserved for garnish

¼ cup chopped fresh mint

Salt and freshly ground black pepper

1 baguette, cut into ¾-inch slices

Olive oil

½ pound burrata

5 almonds, chopped, for garnish

Good-quality extra-virgin olive oil or maple syrup, for finishing

In a bowl, combine the grapefruit and fennel with the mint and carefully fold together. Add salt and pepper to taste and allow the mixture to sit at room temperature or in the fridge for about 30 minutes prior to serving.

Preheat the oven to 400°F.

Make the toast by first brushing the baguette slices with oil, then browning in the oven to your liking.

Top the burrata with the grapefruit-fennel mixture, a pinch of chopped almonds, a couple wisps of fennel frond, and a drizzle of finishing oil. Serve with toasted bread.

SPRING

WHISKEY'D BURRATA TOAST

SERVES 6

---

1 baguette, cut into ¾-inch slices

Olive oil

1 to 2 sprigs fresh rosemary

1 bay leaf

1 tablespoon whole black peppercorns

1 pound sour or regular cherries, pitted (if using regular cherries, halve the sugar)

1 cup sugar

½ cup bourbon, rye, or whiskey

1 tablespoon Scotch, preferably a "peaty" one, such as Islay

Pinch of salt

½ pound burrata

Grated zest of 1 lime

Preheat the oven to 400°F.

Make the toast by first brushing the baguette slices with oil, then placing them in the oven to brown to your liking.

Make a bouquet garni (a tied cheesecloth pouch—see page 251) with the rosemary, bay leaf, and peppercorns.

Place the bouquet garni, cherries, sugar, bourbon, Scotch, and salt in a medium saucepan with ½ cup water. Bring to a boil over medium-high heat, reduce to a simmer, and let everything cook until the cherries have burst and are tender, about 10 minutes. Transfer the cherries to a bowl, but continue simmering the remaining liquid until it reduces to a syrupy consistency, about 15 minutes. Remove from the heat and let cool slightly. Add the cherries back to the syrup.

Top the burrata with the cherry compote and finish with a bit of lime zest. Serve with toasted bread.

SUMMER
TOMATO CONFIT BURRATA TOAST
SERVES 6

1 head of garlic

Salt and freshly ground black pepper

20 cherry tomatoes, halved

Extra-virgin olive oil

Pinch of sugar

Leaves from 3 to 5 sprigs fresh thyme

Leaves from 1 sprig fresh rosemary, roughly chopped

1 baguette, cut into ¾-inch slices

½ pound burrata

Good pinch of thinly sliced fresh basil

Maldon or other flaky salt

Squeeze of lemon

Preheat the oven to 275°F.

Slice the top off the head of garlic. Sprinkle the exposed cloves with salt and pepper, then wrap in foil. Roast until the cloves are completely soft, about 1 hour.

Spread out the tomatoes skin side down on a rimmed baking sheet so that they're all in one layer. Drizzle with oil and season with salt, pepper, sugar, thyme, and rosemary. Roast alongside the garlic until the tomatoes are dark red but still hold their shape, about 45 minutes.

Transfer the tomatoes to a mixing bowl. Add a few cloves of the garlic and a drizzle of oil and a good toss. Check for seasoning and adjust as desired, adding more garlic, salt, and/or pepper.

Raise the oven temperature to 400°F.

Make the toast by brushing the baguette slices with oil, then browning them in the oven.

Spoon the tomato confit over the burrata and sprinkle with fresh basil, Maldon salt, and the lemon juice. Serve with toasted bread.

NOTE: HOW TO SUPREME CITRUS
Supreme *(rhymes with* them*)* is one of those fancy-sounding techniques that makes a big difference in a dish. The basic idea is to free the natural wedges of citrus fruit from the fibrous skins that hold them.
To start, cut the top and bottom off your citrus. With your knife, follow the fruit's natural curve, separating the white part beneath the peel from the flesh. You'll see how the fruit is striped with membrane. Use a paring knife to delicately cut a V shape between each strip, stopping your knife about halfway through the fruit. The supremes will fall away.

"MASTERING" WINE

BYRON BATES

Besides being a longtime friend, Byron Bates is the wine director for the SoHo and Tribeca Grand Hotels and owner of Goatboy Selections, representing organic, biodynamic, and natural winemakers. Having spent many evenings conducting "market research" (i.e., drinking lots of wine) with Byron, I've learned that no one is as passionate about the topic. I'd follow him to the bottom of any glass, and, because he kindly agreed to give us a primer on how to choose wines for yourself, you can, too.

STEP 1: FIGURE OUT WHAT YOU LIKE

Learning about wine is just like checking out new music: It's subjective, broad, diverse, and best done with friends. You learn what you like through experience, not from haughty magazines or critics who tell you what you should be drinking. And at the end of the day, the more you drink, the more you know. That's all it ever should be—not some lofty pleasure for lofty types.

There are many books, classes, publications, and websites out there that will often only make wine more complicated. For the moment, try to ignore them all. There is no way to *read* yourself toward wine mastery. But hopefully we can simplify these matters for you enough to discover some amazing wines you never knew about.

What I always tell people who are looking to get into wine is to find one they like and go from there. Ask yourself, "What do I like about it? The way it smells? The way it feels in my mouth? The flavor?" Try to identify the things about it that you think are delicious. Then start asking around for other wines that show similar characteristics. It's just like when you started exploring bands as a teen—you heard that great single on the radio, listened to it to death, then asked around about what else that group had done or other groups who were similar. Maybe it was the guys at the record store, your older brother, or your friends. You went to someone whose taste you trusted and follow their lead. The same goes for wine, except here you're looking for a good bar, a restaurant whose wine list always delivers, or a wine store whose staff you like.

That said, if you'd like to learn more about wines by yourself, check out the film *Mondovino* by Jonathan Nossiter as well as his book *Liquid Memory*. Other notable books are *How to Love*

Wine by *New York Times* wine critic, Eric Asimov, and *Reading Between the Wines* by importer Terry Theise.

WHY I LIKE MINE NATURAL Natural wine is a movement in the wine world that's all about intervening in the wine as little as possible. You could call natural wine "green wine" or "pure wine" or maybe even "real wine," but whatever term you choose, it's basically just wine that is made from grapes grown using organic or biodynamic methods, then letting wild yeasts ferment the juice with little to no additives, such as sulfur. It is also aged in a vessel that won't impart its flavor on the wine, unlike oak barrels. It's how winemakers let the elements that make wine unique and special—the weather, soil, and local farming tradition, or *terroir*—shine through. All told, natural wine isn't a political statement or environmental movement; it's just a way of making really good, honest wine. Think about how you shop for produce—wouldn't you rather buy tomatoes from the farmer who doesn't bathe his crops in chemicals and takes the utmost care of the land he tends? Or forget sentimentality; that tomato is going to taste a lot better than its commercially farmed, artificially ripened, refrigerated truck-transported counterparts. The same goes for wine. Corporate wineries want to make the same product every year. Consistency is valued a lot higher than things like expression or purity. Think of them as the major record labels of the wine world versus the punk/progressive/indie movement of natural winemaking. These guys aren't going for uniformity from year to year or even bottle to bottle, and they sure as hell aren't going for perfection. But I think that's what makes a much more interesting—and enjoyable—bottle of wine.

| STEP 2: INCREASE YOUR ODDS OF DRINKING A GREAT BOTTLE |

Forget everything you've ever learned *except* white with fish, red with meat. It's not always accurate, but it's pretty close. Another trick is to match the color of the food with the wine: Think salmon with rosé or a skin-macerated white, a simple grilled steak with a light red, cod with a white wine, and a rich, brown stew with a deep, ruby red wine.

Treat importers (domestic and international) like your favorite record labels—if you find you're into bands on a certain label, then there's a good chance other bands on that label will be worth checking out. Good importers usually have a philosophy in their approach to the winemakers they represent, so it's a safe bet that if you like what they do with one kind of wine, you'll like another. To find out who's importing what, simply look on the back side of a bottle. The following importers seldom disappoint me: Kermit Lynch, Louis/Dressner Selections, Rosenthal, Selection Massale, and Weygandt.

At some point in life, you will find yourself in a town with one liquor store and none of the aforementioned importers. It could be best to rethink your dinner pairings and just buy a nice bottle of vodka and your choice of mixer or a standby case of beer. But if you're determined to impress with a bottle of wine, there are some strategies that will help you through even the most dire situations:

- The first rule here is to not spend more than $20 on a bottle in a liquor store. You can't spend your way out of a bad selection. Second, choose a wine with a good-looking label. Why? In this situation you're playing the odds, and judging a wine by its label can actually increase those odds. Think of it as aesthetic instinct—the same way a cool label attracts you to a band or record. If you like the label, there's a better chance the winemaker's style will suit you.

- From there, look for grapes nobody's ever heard of from regions that are an afterthought to most retailers. Wines from more mainstream locales tend to be overpriced and are often factory-produced. Is this always the case? No, but we're increasing our odds again.

- So if you want bubbles, look for Cava or Prosecco. If you want something white, look for a wine from Spain, Portugal, southern Italy, or the South of France. If you see Muscadet or Albariño, grab it. For red, Beaujolais is always a good bet. These wines are simple, delightful, pure, and rarely offensive. In particular, look for Morgon, Beaujolais-Villages, or Brouilly. Also, look to the Loire Valley for great, inexpensive reds. Chinon, Bourgueil, or Saumur-Champigny are some options.

- As for American wines, the same rules apply—look for regions that are off the beaten path: the Finger Lakes (New York); Central Coast, Mendocino, and Santa Barbara (California); Willamette Valley (Oregon); and Yakima Valley (Washington), just to list a few. Also, keep your eyes peeled for these producers who have yet to let me down: Dashe, Nalle, Truchard, Sinskey, Edmunds St. John, Fetzer, Ravenswood, and Ridge.

If you can't find what you want locally and have the time to plan ahead, ordering online is a fantastic option. Check out Wine.com, WineCommune.com, and ChambersStWines.com and apply aforementioned rules. These sites offer incredible service and will deliver to most states.

You don't need crystal stemware and a temperature-controlled wine refrigerator to do a wine justice. That's one of the beautiful things about buying natural wine—it's a humble tipple meant for convivial consumption, not white-glove service. Regardless of what you're drinking, though, just a few simple steps will ensure you're getting to the bottom of the bottle as enjoyably as possible:

• Get the wine to the right temperature. Serving white wine too cold or red wine too warm can destroy some of the nuance of the wine. The ideal temperature is 50° to 55°F, but if you don't have a special wine refrigerator, just keep both your reds and whites in the fridge. Pull them out about an hour before serving and enjoy them a little colder than room temperature.

• Transfer the wine to a carafe or decanter. Especially if it's a wine made without sulfites or other additives, this will allow it to blow off some of the carbon dioxide that naturally accumulates in the bottle, or "shake the fizz out." In a nutshell, it'll taste better.

• Pour it in the right glass. We're not talking Riedel here. If you're drinking for enjoyment, and again, especially if you're enjoying a bottle of natural wine, any glassware will do. Old Ball jars, juice glasses, or highball glasses are all perfect. When serving a sparkling wine, however, I recommend something closer to a white-wine glass, with a narrow body and smaller opening at the mouth, which keeps the delicate essences of the wine concentrated in the glass. That said, you're welcome to forget the traditional flute—it's not the *only* glass for sparkling varietals.

• Enjoy it. The best way to do that is to stop treating it like a luxury item. We're not analyzing a Wagner movement. We're tuning in to the FM college radio station at 3 a.m. while your roommates are baking brownies. No rules, no candles. It's just a bottle of wine—so enjoy it.

DINNER 3

Pan-Seared Squid

Butternut Squash Puree

Wild Rice with Celery and Pecans

**Carrot, Parsley, and Pomegranate Salad
with Confit Shallot Vinaigrette**

Lemon Verbena Tart

TO DRINK

Dry, sparkling white wine, such as a Crémant du Jura
or dry Riesling from Alsace—something very light
that won't overpower the squid

PAN-SEARED SQUID

SERVES 4 TO 6

Squid is one of those things that people think they can have only if they're eating in a restaurant. We get it. They're kind of scary to take home because they look like little alien things that should probably be left to the pros. The truth is that squid couldn't be easier to prepare and cook (especially if you do leave the cleaning to the pros—ask your fishmonger to do this for you).

---

6 medium squid (about 4 ounces each)

Olive oil

Salt and freshly ground black pepper

1 generous tablespoon unsalted butter

Extra-virgin olive oil

Coarse sea salt

Squeeze of lemon

Lay each squid flat on your cutting board. The goal here is to open them up like a fillet. First locate the "seam" that runs down the side of the body, like the stitching on a pair of jeans. Gently run your knife along the seam, then cut the body again lengthwise so you have two halves.

Situate each piece on your cutting board so that what was once the inside is facing up. Now score each fillet with gentle knife cuts to help the heat distribute more evenly and make the squid more tender. Gently run the blade of your knife across the top of the squid flesh in diagonal lines about ¼ inch apart or less. Be careful not to cut all the way through the flesh. Repeat with diagonal lines running the opposite angle so that you create what looks like a diamond pattern.

Place the scored squid in a large bowl and toss with olive oil to coat, salt, and pepper.

Heat a large cast-iron skillet over a medium-high flame. You want it hot but not smoking. Add enough olive oil to just coat the bottom of the skillet, then place the squid nonscored side down. Cook only as much as will fit comfortably in one layer. Once the squid begin to curl up after about 30 seconds, flip the fillets and allow them to fully curl onto themselves, pressing them gently with a spoon so they stay in contact with the skillet. Add the legs (if using) and cook until the squid is golden brown, 1 to 2 minutes total. Be careful not to overcook your squid.

Once the squid is just about done, add the butter, let it foam, then *arroser* (see page 251), basting until the squid is a tad firmer than a sponge but not much.

Remove the squid from the skillet and let drain for a moment on paper towel. Finish with a bit of extra-virgin olive oil, sea salt, and lemon juice.

BUTTERNUT SQUASH PUREE

MAKES 3 CUPS

This puree is one of our favorites because squash is an inexpensive vegetable that gives off a deep, rich flavor with very little effort. These massive gourds can look a little intimidating at the market, but there's really nothing to getting into them. You can save the seeds to roast later since they have a nice, nutty flavor and add crunchy texture to a dish. Just rinse the squash fibers off them, pat dry, toss in a little bit of olive oil, spread them on a baking sheet, and roast at 400°F for about 7 minutes, until they are golden and crisp.

---

1 butternut squash, peeled and cubed

4 cups milk

2 cups heavy cream

1 head of garlic, top sliced off, exposing the cloves

4 sprigs fresh thyme

6 whole black peppercorns

Salt

First, cut off the stem and root ends of the squash to make it more stable for chopping. Then peel off the skin with a vegetable peeler or small knife. Next, cut lengthwise down the center of the squash. Use a spoon and scoop out the seeds and fibrous strands from inside—now you just have to chop it into whichever size pieces you need. A general rule of thumb is the smaller the size, the sweeter the taste after it's cooked, because there's more surface area to caramelize.

In a large saucepan, cover the squash with the milk and cream. Make a bouquet garni (see page 251) with the garlic, thyme, and peppercorns and throw it into the pot. Over medium-high heat, bring the contents to a boil, then reduce heat to a simmer. Gently cook until the squash yields easily to a fork or cake tester, about 20 minutes.

Strain the mixture, reserving the liquid and discarding the bouquet. Add the squash to a food processor and blend until smooth, adding some of the cooking liquid to adjust the consistency. It should be just thick enough that a spoonful held upside down holds for half a second before falling. Season with salt to taste.

WILD RICE
WITH CELERY AND PECANS

SERVES 4 TO 6

1 generous tablespoon unsalted butter

1 shallot, diced

Salt

1 garlic clove, grated

Pinch of crushed red pepper flakes

1 teaspoon ground cumin

½ cup dry white wine (something you'd be okay drinking)

2 cups vegetable stock

1 cup wild rice

1 stalk celery, peeled, diced, and small leaves reserved for garnish (you can skip peeling if you want, but we like how it makes the celery less stringy)

½ cup pecans, crushed and toasted (see page 255)

Freshly ground black pepper

Heat a medium saucepan over low heat, add the butter, and let it heat until it just begins to foam. Add the shallot and allow it to sweat until translucent, about 3 minutes. Season with a pinch of salt and the garlic, red pepper flakes, and cumin. Continue sweating the mixture for another 2 minutes.

Add the wine and bring to a boil over medium-high heat. Allow the liquid to reduce for 1 minute. Add the stock and again bring to a boil. Stir in the rice, reduce the heat to medium, and cover. Check to make sure the rice is bubbling gently. If it is at a wild boil, reduce the heat. Cook for about 20 minutes, or until the rice is tender and has absorbed all the liquid.

Fold in the celery and pecans, season with salt and pepper to taste, and garnish with the celery leaves.

LEFTOVERS

STUFFED POBLANOS
WITH EGGS AND ANNA'S CHILI SAUCE

SERVES 4

If you've made the Wild Rice with Celery and Pecans (above)—or any other grain-based dish in this book, for that matter—and find yourself with a bunch of leftovers, there's no better way to recycle it than by stuffing it into a roasted poblano pepper with an egg on top and spicy, creamy chili sauce.

Grapeseed or canola oil

2 poblano peppers

Salt

2 cups leftover grains such as rice, quinoa, or farro

4 large eggs

Anna's Chili Sauce, to taste (recipe follows)

Preheat the oven to 350°F.

Heat a large cast-iron skillet until it's smoking hot. Coat the bottom with oil and add the peppers, letting them char on all sides. Remove from the skillet and allow to cool enough to handle.

Cut the peppers in half and remove the seeds.

Gently season the inside of the peppers with salt and fill each one with a scoop of rice. Make a small well in the rice, and lay the peppers on a baking sheet.

Crack an egg into each well, season the eggs with salt, and transfer the peppers to the oven. Cook for about 15 minutes or until the whites have set but the yolks are still runny (they should still be bright in color).

To finish, dress with the chili sauce.

ANNA'S CHILI SAUCE

MAKES 1 CUP

Our friend Anna is our matriarch of spice. We have never met anyone who can handle spicy food the way she can. On multiple occasions, we've watched as she asked for a second or third side of hot sauce, poured it over her food, and downed it while servers stare back in disbelief. When she first made this sauce, it was a revelation. We started putting it on everything we could think of and had to share it in this book. That said, we toned it down a little—'cause not all of us are Anna. Feel free to pour this stuff on your eggs, potatoes, tacos, chicken, fish—you name it. You can make this sauce using any store-bought chili powder, but Anna highly recommends you seek out one made in New Mexico.

---

6 tablespoons olive oil

½ cup chopped red onion

2 large garlic cloves, chopped

Pinch of salt

¼ cup red chili powder

1 teaspoon ground cumin

1 teaspoon smoked paprika

1 teaspoon mustard powder

Warm 2 tablespoons of the oil in a medium sauté pan over medium heat. Add the onion, garlic, and salt and cook until the onions are soft and lightly browned, but not completely caramelized, about 10 minutes. Add the chili powder and ½ cup water. Mix with a spoon or whisk to form a thin paste, making sure to scrape up any ingredients sticking to the bottom of the pan. Keep the sauce barely simmering over low heat and stir in the cumin, paprika, and mustard powder. Add the remaining oil a couple of tablespoons at a time. Move the pan so it's only partially over the heat and continue stirring, adding a little water at a time until you've reached a creamy consistency, about 20 minutes. Remove from the heat, let cool completely, and serve or store in the fridge.

CARROT, PARSLEY, AND POMEGRANATE SALAD
WITH CONFIT SHALLOT VINAIGRETTE

SERVES 4

Combining the bright crispness of carrots with the tartness of pomegranate, this salad is much more fun than your average carrot slaw. Parsley adds some herbal freshness to the mix, and when combined with the caramely confit-sweetened shallots, this becomes a perfectly balanced dish that pairs well with seafood, especially squid. Plus, you can make the super-simple vinaigrette ahead of time and store leftovers in the fridge for up to a week for quick salads.

FOR THE VINAIGRETTE

2 shallots

¼ cup extra-virgin olive oil

Salt

⅓ cup champagne vinegar

Freshly ground black pepper

FOR THE SALAD

4 medium or 8 small carrots

½ bunch fresh parsley

½ pomegranate

½ cup pumpkin seeds or pistachios, toasted (optional)

Make the vinaigrette: Preheat the oven to 225°F. Grab your shallots and trim off both ends (the root and the tip)—no need to peel. Place them on a piece of foil big enough to wrap them completely, coat them in oil, and throw on a little salt. Make a little packet with the foil and place in the oven for 1 to 1½ hours, until they have completely softened. Once done, allow them to cool, then squeeze them out of their skin and transfer to a blender. Combine the shallots with the vinegar and oil to taste, following our vinaigrette method (see page 107). Season with salt and pepper to taste.

Make the salad: Slice the carrots as thinly as possible lengthwise. If you have a mandoline, this is a good time to use it.

Pick the leaves of parsley from the thicker stems and wash, as you would greens. No need to chop the leaves, just serve them whole.

For the pomegranate, the easiest way to pull the seeds from the white membrane is to do it with your hands, underwater. This will keep the seeds from flying around the kitchen, so you can feed your friends and not just the dog.

In a medium bowl, mix the carrots, parsley, pomegranate, and pumpkin seeds (if using). Season the mixture with salt and pepper and then dress to taste with the shallot vinaigrette.

LEMON VERBENA TART

SERVES 6 TO 8

Lemon verbena is a leafy herb with a strong lemon flavor. It's really easy to grow in a sunny spot in your garden, but because it's probably hard to find fresh in the grocery store, you're better off buying the dried herb, which is commonly sold as an herbal tea. The verbena gives a more intense, rich flavor to this tart, which would otherwise be a classic lemon tart recipe.

FOR THE SWEET PASTRY

9 tablespoons unsalted butter, cold, cut into small pieces, plus more for greasing the pan

Scant 1 cup (3.2 ounces) powdered sugar

1 large egg

2 cups (8.8 ounces) all-purpose flour

FOR THE LEMON VERBENA FILLING

1 cup light cream

10 fresh or dried lemon verbena leaves

4 large eggs

6 tablespoons (2.5 ounces) granulated sugar

Juice of 2 lemons

1 cup crème fraîche, for serving

SPECIAL EQUIPMENT

8-inch tart pan with removable bottom; pie weights or 1 16-ounce bag dried beans; pastry brush

Make the dough: Place the butter and powdered sugar in a food processor and mix until combined. Add the egg and process for another 20 seconds. Add the flour and process for a few seconds more until the mixture comes together. If it seems dry, add 1 or 2 teaspoons cold water, one teaspoon at a time. You don't want to add too much water, or the dough will get sticky and hard to roll out; use just enough to make a ball of dough come together. Turn out the dough on a work surface dusted with flour and knead just to incorporate. Shape the dough into a disk, cover with plastic wrap, and refrigerate for at least 30 minutes.

Make the filling and tart: Place the cream in a pot over low heat and slowly bring to a simmer. Stir in the lemon verbena leaves, then take off the heat. Let steep for 20 minutes to infuse.

Preheat the oven to 350°F.

Once the pastry has rested, grease the tart pan with softened butter. Dust the pan lightly with flour, tapping out any excess.

On a floured work surface, roll out the dough so that it's just large enough to fill the tart pan with an inch or two extra hanging over the side.

Refrigerate for 20 minutes and return to the filling.

Whisk together 3 eggs and the granulated sugar in a medium bowl. When the infused cream has cooled slightly, stir it into the egg-sugar mixture. Add the lemon juice and strain the mixture through a fine-meshed sieve to get rid of the verbena leaves. Set aside.

Remove the now-rested pastry dough from the fridge and trim away any excess that hangs over the side of the pan. Use a fork to prick the dough all over, or "dock" the pastry, which will help keep the dough from rising. Line the top of the dough with parchment paper and top with enough pie weights to fill the tart pan. This will also keep the dough from puffing up as it bakes. Put the tart shell into the oven and bake until the bottom is cooked and slightly golden, about 15 minutes. Remove the pie weights and parchment paper. Whisk the remaining egg and brush the base of the tart with it to seal off any holes or cracks that might allow the filling to run. Slowly fill the crust with the filling.

Lower the oven to 250°F. Bake for 30 minutes, or until the filling has a slight wobble in the center. Remove from the oven and leave to cool completely at room temperature. Serve with crème fraîche.

THE HOME BAR

NINO CIRABISI

Here's the problem with having a friend like Nino: His drinks are too good. Every time we're hanging out, without fail, we end up drinking a little more than we intended because, well, we can't help throwing back whatever he's putting down. We're pretty pumped to tell you that you're about to have the same problem because we're going to bring a little bit of Nino Cirabisi—who's been working in the New York cocktail scene for more than ten years—into your home. You're welcome and we're sorry.

I can't count the number of parties I've attended where the "bar" is nothing more than a corner of the kitchen counter jammed with random bottles of spirits, a few loose wedges of citrus rolling around next to a melted bag of ice, and a high-tech wine opener that no one seems to know how to use. After twenty years of being behind the bar, I do what any good barman would when confronted with this scene: I look in the fridge for beer.

It doesn't have to be this way, though. With just a few basic tools, a little technique, and the right selection of spirits, anyone can have a home bar that is sure to impress.

| TOOLS |

You don't need to go out and buy a complete bar set. I've stirred plenty of drinks with a loose chopstick or muddled fruit with the end of a wooden spoon, but here are some items that you might want to have around. I've chosen things that I feel are the simplest to use, have stood the test of time, and serve multiple purposes.

1. SHAKER AND MIXING GLASS: There are many styles and variations of shakers ranging from ornate Parisian versions to three-piece cobblers with built-in strainers. My choice is the Boston shaker, which is simply a mixing tin and a clear pint glass—I like that you can see what you're building in it. Plus, if you go that route, there's no need to buy an additional mixing glass—especially not a fancy Japanese crystal one.

2. STRAINER: There are two types of strainers: a Hawthorne and a julep. The pronged Hawthorne—the kind with a springlike coil at one end—is used mostly to strain shaken drinks

from a tin, and a colander-like julep is used for stirred drinks poured from a glass. Just go with the Hawthorne strainer, as it fits over both glasses and tins.

3. JIGGERS: Jiggers are to bartenders what measuring cups are to bakers and chefs. The best are the two-sided versions. You'll never need more than two: 1 ounce / 2 ounce and a ½ ounce / ¾ ounce.

4. BAR SPOON: The long, metal, twisted-stem kind you see in cocktail bars are great for stirring drinks without breaking the ice, which can dilute and cloud a drink. Also, it looks really cool when you learn how to stir it correctly. We'll get to that later.

5. MUDDLER: These come in all shapes and sizes, but I like a fairly heavy wooden muddler to gently press and express the oils and juices from your ingredients. But remember to take it easy; you're not making pesto or venting sexual frustration.

6. CITRUS PRESS: Fresh juice will make a world of difference to any drink you make. You can use a citrus press to squeeze it straight into your mixing glass or jigger. And if you plan to make a lot of drinks, this will make your life a lot easier—you'll be able to prep a few bottles of fresh juice ahead of time much more efficiently. I recommend the classic elbow-grease tabletop press. Electric juicers take off too much pith and pulp, which can make your citrus juice taste bitter.

7. ICE-CUBE TRAYS: The right shape and size of ice is an essential part of making a great drink: It's all about controlling how fast it melts and having the right temperature and level of dilution. I recommend silicone ice trays in two sizes: 1¼-inch cubes for tall drinks, shaking, and stirring; 2-inch cubes for spirits on the rocks and boozy cocktails like an old-fashioned.

8. BAR RAG: Keeping a clean, dry towel around is always advised. Someone will spill something. I promise. And it's multipurpose—fill the center of the towel with ice, fold it closed, and beat the hell out of it with your muddler. Ta-da! Crushed ice for juleps!

9. WINE KEY: Not a corkscrew or wall-mounted electric wine opener—those are for people who don't actually drink or, worse, spend all night talking about what they're drinking. A wine key is easy to use and has the bonus of a beer bottle opener and a foil knife.

10. POUR SPOUTS: The long, narrow stainless-steel kind helps control your pours, especially after you've had a few. Use your jiggers to practice counting measurements: A quick count to two while pouring and you should have ½ ounce, four gives you 1 ounce, and eight is 2 ounces. You'll be moonlighting in no time.

| TECHNIQUE |

Regardless of what you put in a cocktail, *how* you make it matters: The idea is to control the temperature, dilution, aeration, and flavor. The three basic techniques for making cocktails achieve this each in their own way. Let's take a look at them now:

SHAKING: Here we chill a drink by shaking it with ice. This also aids in dilution, because the ice breaks down by the force of shaking, and the little shards of ice melt quickly. Aeration takes place as well, as you add air bubbles to the drink. Shaking is used primarily with drinks that include juices, creams, eggs, or anything else that is not a spirit. That is, except for carbonated ingredients. That just makes a mess. When shaking a drink you want to put some elbow grease into it. The idea is to shake the drink awake, not rock it to sleep. Slap the shaker onto the mixing glass with some force, and give the drink a good go for 15 to 20 seconds.

STIRRING: When you're making a drink that contains all alcoholic ingredients or clear ingredients, it is usually stirred. This is to ensure that the drink does not become too diluted, is chilled without being clouded with too much air, and that the flavor remains clean and crisp. The key is stirring smoothly and gently. Place the bar spoon in the ice-filled glass and swirl with the back of the spoon touching the inside of the glass for 20 to 30 seconds. The technique is to curl your fingers around the stem and twirl it so that it spins around the glass. (This is where you'll find the twisted stem really handy.) You want to make sure the ice and cocktail spin around without cracking the ice or frothing up the drink. The drink should be cold and the ice should have melted slightly.

BUILDING: Building a drink takes place in the glass it is served in. The ingredients are added to the glass and stirred with a straw. Most often you do this with drinks that include carbonated mixers. A gin and tonic, screwdriver, and rum and Coke are all built drinks.

| STOCKING YOUR BAR |

You don't need to go out and buy dozens of bottles of booze to have a well-stocked bar. I suggest approaching this the way you would prepare a meal: You get the ingredients you need to make one dish and then add to the leftovers to make another meal. Let's say you enjoy a rye old-fashioned. Pick up some rye and Angostura bitters, make some simple syrup (more on that later), and you've got what you need. Then you might want to look at other rye cocktails you're interested in and can make with ingredients you have plus one or two others. For example, a Manhattan is nothing more than an old-fashioned with sweet vermouth instead of simple syrup. Many cocktails are as easy as switching the base alcohol or adding and subtracting a few things.

In choosing base spirits, I think it best to look at their characteristics instead of rattling off name brands. Here are the five that are the foundation of any bar:

GIN: I like a London Dry–style gin. It's full of juniper and the bold flavor comes through in many cocktails.

LIGHT RUM: I could write an entire book on rum, but it's been done already. Let's keep it simple—light rum is made with sugarcane. Find one that tastes like it! Or at least strike a good balance between sweetness and proof—not firewater and not sugary sweet. I like the sweet characteristics that can be compared to dessert ingredients, such as vanilla, caramel, and molasses.

TEQUILA: Always look for one that's 100 percent agave. Then it's just a matter of taste. I like my tequila to have some round, rich, smooth, and earthy characteristics. For this I choose a Reposado (tequila that's been aged for two months to a year). If you like yours with some kick and sharp, crisp flavor, go with an unaged Blanco or Plata.

WHISKEY: Rye or bourbon? Depends on what you like. Whichever it is, I think it should be close to 100 proof. More bounce to ounce, pinch to the inch, or any other fun way to say it's stronger and therefore features better in cocktails. Rye is made with a minimum of 51 percent rye and bourbon is made with a minimum of 51 percent corn, so like bread, rye has a spicier, more peppery flavor and bourbon tends to be sweeter with notes of vanilla.

MODIFIER SPIRITS: I call the following "modifier spirits" because they are most commonly added to base spirits to create a cocktail, though they can be enjoyed on their own as well:

• **AMARI:** Here's where you need to listen and trust because it can get confusing. An amaro is an Italian herbal liqueur that's usually drunk as a digestif (after dinner). Italian booze? Fancy French terms? Aahhhhh! Basically, this category includes all the bittersweet, funny-colored, funky spirits from around the world that are derived from herbs, roots, bark, citrus, and all sorts of other crazy stuff. These include Averna, Montenegro, Jägermeister, and Becherovka. I also include Campari and Aperol in this group even though they're considered aperitifs (before dinner). Why? Because I can. And for our home bar purposes I'm also including Fernet. Fernet is what every bartender in all the fancy cocktail bars drink. You'll see them taking shots of it with friends and other bartenders while complimenting each other's vests and mustaches. I'm counting it here instead of in our five-base spirits, though. My cocktail chapter, my rules. Clearly this is going to my head.

- **VERMOUTHS:** These are fortified wines that are native to northern Italy and southern France and sometimes include herbs. The simplest way to distinguish them from one another is: dry (white) and sweet (red). Look at them like bottles of wine and try to find one of each that you like. Cook with them, drink them alone on the rocks, and whatever you do, keep them refrigerated and covered. It's wine and even though it's fortified to last over time, it will expire.

- I also include in this category any spirits that have a single strong flavor characteristic that might be overwhelming on its own, such as cassis, flavored liqueurs, and maraschino.

Now let's get to some fun things we can do to add new and interesting flavors to our cocktails:

SYRUPS: All bars use "simple syrup." All it is, is 1 part water to 1 part sugar, heated until the sugar dissolves. Make a bottle of it and keep it in the fridge. If you add a couple of drops of vodka to it, it will keep for up to a month. With this basic recipe you can create any number of flavored syrups by infusing it with other ingredients like vanilla, cinnamon, cardamom, raspberries, and so on. Just pour your hot simple syrup over the additional ingredients and let steep for a few hours, depending on how much flavor you want. Strain the syrup and keep in the fridge.

JUICES: The basic bar always has fresh lemon and lime juice. Depending on how many drinks you're making, it might help to squeeze some beforehand.

BITTERS: There's been quite a craze recently of people making their own and there are some really unique boutique bitters on the market. Many of them are fantastic but for the home bar I recommend the three classics: Angostura, Peychauds, and Regans' orange bitters. Look them up, try them, and get familiar with how they taste. They are essential to making many classic cocktails and are brilliant for the level of depth and balance they bring to a drink. Angostura has also been known to help alleviate a stomachache and cure the hiccups, common symptoms from overimbibing.

| MIXING IT ALL TOGETHER |

So now let's make some great-tasting drinks! How? By understanding what it is we taste. Sweet, sour, salty, bitter, spicy, savory—all of the things we think of when describing food come into play when making a cocktail. Let's take a look at some classic drinks, see how they balance flavors, and see how we can play with them:

Let's start with the **NEGRONI:** 1 ounce gin, 1 ounce Campari, 1 ounce sweet vermouth. Stir with ice and strain into a glass over fresh ice. Garnish with an orange peel. This is a wonderful drink because it balances the bitter of the Campari with the sweetness of the vermouth, and the gin gives it a clean, crisp note.

Now, if you make the same drink with rye instead of gin? You have a **BOULEVARDIER**. Serve it straight up, or with no ice. Here the rye is providing a spicy kick. Use dry vermouth instead of sweet vermouth in the Boulevardier and you've got an **OLD PAL**. Now the sweetness is much more restrained, giving you a leaner, spicier but still aromatic drink, and the Campari's sweetness is more of a balancing note than a dominant one.

During the summer I make a Negroni without gin and top it with club soda. That's called an **AMERICANO**. Bubbles make it more refreshing, and a little easier to handle without the gin. Swap the club soda for sparkling wine and you've got a **SBAGLIATO**, and a crisper, leaner drink.

Let's start with another drink and make that **RYE OLD-FASHIONED**, which consists of 2 ounces rye, ½ ounce simple syrup, 2 to 3 dashes of Angostura bitters. (If you decide to use bourbon instead, I'd use a touch less syrup because bourbon tends to be sweeter.) Stir with ice and strain into a glass over fresh ice. Garnish with an orange and lemon peel. Again, this drink works because the sugar and bitters balance each other plus the spicy kick of the rye, and the citrus peels give a bit of refreshing aroma.

Now, if you take away the simple syrup and replace it with 1 ounce sweet vermouth, you have a **MANHATTAN**. These are served straight up with a good-quality brandied cherry. This is more complex, aroma-wise, than the old-fashioned, but some people find the Manhattan on the sweet side. If you agree, try making it instead with ½ ounce sweet vermouth and ½ ounce dry vermouth. That's a **PERFECT MANHATTAN**. The dry vermouth alleviates the sweetness but still brings floral character.

Want to shake something, you say? Okay, let's make a simple **DAIQUIRI**: 2 ounces rum, ¾ ounce lime juice, ½ ounce simple syrup. Shake all of the ingredients with ice and strain, straight up, into a cocktail glass. Sugar and lime juice. Sweet and sour. *Balance.* That's the key to this classic. Bartenders know that every drink that is a "sour" contains some combination of sweetness to go with the acidity. The origins of these kinds of drinks probably stem from sailors drinking rum with lime juice to ward off scurvy. They added sugar to make it more palatable, which works with all sorts of citrus.

Muddle some mint into your daiquiri and you have a **MOJITO**. And a daiquri with tequila instead of rum? That's a **MARGARITA**. Put some salt on the rim for another way to stimulate the taste buds. Or swap the rum for bourbon and the lime juice for lemon to make a **WHISKEY SOUR**. That's 2 ounces bourbon, ¾ ounce lemon juice, ½ ounce simple syrup. Shake with ice and strain into a glass with fresh ice. Garnish with an orange slice and a cherry. We could also add an egg white to it and shake it really hard to froth it up and give it a different mouthfeel.

Same thing goes for a **TOM COLLINS**, which is pretty much a gin sour with club soda—it works because of the balance of sweet and sour. Now if we added an egg white to that, a little orange flower water, and heavy cream, you've got a **RAMOS GIN FIZZ**. Adding that one extra element just brings a different taste experience that is held together with the balance of the sour and sweet.

A **CLOVER CLUB** is 2 ounces gin, ½ ounce lemon juice, ½ ounce raspberry syrup, and 1 egg white. Shake hard with ice and strain into a cocktail glass. It's a sour foundation with the egg white added for a smooth mouthfeel, and the raspberry gives it another unique dimension. Hell, I just throw a few raspberries in with regular simple syrup and shake that all up. It's still a good drink. Remember that mojito I mentioned earlier? That's basically a sour with another element added to it, and there's no reason why you can't play around with other ingredients. I started making mojitos with rye and bitters instead of rum after seeing a bartender at one of my favorite bars do just the same and call it an **EX-PATRIOT**.

Now that you have a little understanding of not only how to make these drinks but also how they work, don't be a slave to a recipe. Try switching the base spirit to rum, tequila, and so forth. And how about doing it with the Regans' orange bitters? Or if you like an amaro on the list, use that instead of vermouth and/or bitters for a richer, more complex drink. For example, try this: Remember that Fernet? Okay, stir together 2 ounces rye, ½ ounce Fernet, ¼ ounce simple syrup, and 2 to 3 dashes of Angostura bitters. Serve it up with a lemon peel and it's a **TORONTO**. Yes, the Fernet is bitter and medicinal, but it's also a bit sweet, so we've cut down on the simple syrup.

The key here is *balance*. Sweetness balances bitterness. Sour things balance sweetness. Carbonation lightens, shaken egg whites enrich. Every element adds something to the mix that can be balanced by something else. As you taste and make drinks, you'll develop your own preferences and instincts for how to balance them.

The next time you have a drink you really enjoy, ask yourself, "What is it about this drink that I like? What do I taste?" You'll start to figure out what it is you enjoy and you'll have a better understanding of how to make good drinks of your own.

DINNER 4

Clams in Bacon-Mushroom Broth

————

Sautéed Snap Peas and Mushrooms
with Soft-Boiled Eggs

————

Radish Salad with Bottarga

————

Apple Tarte Tatin

WHAT TO DRINK

Dry, sparkling rosé; Lambrusco;
or a white wine from Alsace, such as Sylvaner

CLAMS
IN BACON-MUSHROOM BROTH
SERVES 4

We like making this soup in the fall because it's smoky and warm yet light. Its earthy mushroom flavor, layered with the smoke of bacon, Scotch, and soy sauce will make you never want to eat soup out of a can ever again. If you want to make this dish a little heartier—and take advantage of the root-veg bounty at the markets—we recommend throwing in some baby turnips.

---

4 cups Bacon-Mushroom Broth
(recipe follows)

2 cups mushrooms, such as shiitakes, wiped clean of any dirt, stemmed, and sliced thin

12 littleneck clams or 20 fresh cockles, scrubbed (see Note)

4 small turnips, quartered (optional)

Grapeseed or vegetable oil

8 Brussels sprouts, quartered

Salt and freshly ground black pepper

1 lemon

1 tablespoon thinly sliced fresh chives or scallions (green parts only)

NOTE: COCKLES
While littleneck clams are easy to find and suit this dish perfectly, if you have access to fresh cockles, go with those. They are smaller, but have bigger flavor that's sweet, briny, and just a touch less salty. It's shellfish at its best. Either way, make sure you're buying clams or cockles that are all about the same size so they take the same amount of time to cook.

Add the broth to a large saucepan and bring to a simmer over a medium flame.

Throw your mushrooms, clams, and turnips (if using them) into the soup. Bring the pot back to a simmer and cook until all the mollusks open, 2 to 4 minutes—keep an eye on them. Discard any that won't open. They're goners.

While you're waiting for the clams or cockles to open, coat the bottom of a large heavy-bottomed sauté pan with oil and get it smoking hot over medium-high heat. Add the Brussels sprouts, sprinkle them with just a pinch of salt and pepper, and let them sear until you have some serious char. Remove from the pan and throw them in the bottom of the bowls you'll be serving the soup in.

Taste your broth for seasoning, and if necessary, salt to taste.

Divide soup and clams into the bowls. Finish with lemon zest—just a couple strokes with a Microplane over each bowl—and a pinch of chives or scallions.

BACON-MUSHROOM BROTH

MAKES 4 TO 5 QUARTS OF STOCK

It takes some time to make this broth, but the rewards of a clear, deep-flavored, versatile, and rich broth make the effort well worth it. We rely on it to braise vegetables like baby fennel, just about anything in the onion family, and most root vegetables, especially small potatoes (see page 145). Or you can reduce the stock further, throw in some Parmesan, toss with penne, and have a simple but rich mushroom pasta.

---

6 12-ounce packages of button mushrooms, wiped clean of any dirt and sliced into ¼-inch pieces.

1 medium white onion, roughly chopped

½ pound slab bacon, cut into 1-inch cubes

Salt

Soy sauce

Splash of Scotch, preferably a "peaty" one, such as Islay

Fill an 8-quart stockpot with water. Add half the mushrooms to the water and bring it to a boil over high heat. Reduce your heat and let the broth simmer until it tastes like mushrooms, 45 minutes to 1 hour. Strain out the mushrooms and discard.

Add the second batch of mushrooms along with the onion to the pot, raise the heat to high, and bring the broth back to a boil. Reduce the heat and allow the broth to simmer again, for another 45 minutes. At this point it should taste *and* smell like mushrooms. Strain out the mushrooms and onion and discard.

Add the bacon, bring the broth to a boil over high heat, then once again reduce the heat and let simmer for 30 minutes, or until it takes on the bacon's flavor. Make sure you skim the fat as the bacon simmers. Anything that looks like oil floating on top of the water should get skimmed out into a bowl with a spoon. Lots of stock recipes suggest you simply peel off the solidified fat after you've chilled the stock. It's a good technique, but letting that fat sit on top of the liquid as it cooks also lets some of it emulsify into the broth. Skimming is a labor of love, but this is what will make the difference between a soup that's clean and smoky versus one that's heavy and greasy. Just take a look at the liquid you're removing—it is cloudy and milky, whereas your soup will be a clear brown. Discard the bacon.

Season the broth with salt and a few table-spoons of soy sauce, to taste. You want a faint hint of the soy sauce to add depth to the other flavors. If needed, add more, but do so carefully because you don't want the soy flavor to dominate. Try to undersalt somewhat, so that you can reduce the broth or use it to braise other food in without it getting too salty. (Season it to taste if serving directly.) Add a splash of the Scotch, again just to add enough smokiness to complement the other ingredients.

Serve hot, or let cool and chill in the refrigerator. It will keep in the fridge for about 1 week or in the freezer pretty much indefinitely.

SAUTÉED SNAP PEAS
AND MUSHROOMS WITH SOFT-BOILED EGGS
SERVES 6

This warm salad is the perfect example of how going to the market can be the ultimate inspiration. Just before the farm stands go quiet for colder months, you are able to get the most exciting array of vegetables flavored by the warmth of summer, now finishing their growing season with the cooling temperatures of the coming fall. This is a great dish for transitioning to heartier cold-weather food and also for getting comfortable with eyeballing measurements because nothing has to be too precise—and it's great practice for getting that perfectly runny soft-boiled egg that you can throw on top of pretty much anything.

¾ pound wild mushrooms

½ pound sugar snap peas

Grapeseed or vegetable oil

Salt and freshly ground black pepper

1 small bunch squash runners, cut in half (optional; see Note)

6 large eggs, at room temperature

½ cup chicken stock

2 tablespoons unsalted butter, cold, cut into ½-inch pieces

6 to 12 thin slices of prosciutto

1 lemon

Smoked sea salt or coarse sea salt

NOTE: SQUASH RUNNERS
Squash runners, also known as squash vines, show up at farmers' markets in the fall. They are a cool alternative to other greens and have a sweet green, yet slightly bitter flavor, which goes really well with the mushrooms and prosciutto. If you can't find them, it's okay to simply omit them.

Clean the wild mushrooms. They can be gritty, so take the time to make sure they're free of dirt by wiping them with a damp towel. Cut the mushrooms into uniform bite-size pieces so they'll cook evenly, and if you're using different kinds, keep them separate. Prep the peas by breaking off the tough stems.

Over high heat, generously coat the bottom of a large skillet with oil and heat until it shimmers. Add as many mushrooms as will fit comfortably in one layer—crowding the skillet will cause them to steam, not sear, so cook in batches if necessary. If you're working with different types of mushrooms, cook each kind separately, since their varying textures and shapes cause them to cook differently.

(recipe continues)

When the mushrooms have browned on one side, toss and sear the other side. Season with salt and pepper, taste, and season more if necessary. Once you're done cooking all the mushrooms, set them aside. In the same skillet, add more oil to coat the bottom and heat until it begins to smoke. Add the peas and the squash runners (if using)—remembering not to crowd them too much—season with salt and pepper, and cook until they are nicely charred but still have a bit of snap, 30 seconds to 1 minute. Remove from the skillet and set aside.

In a large saucepan, bring enough water to cover the eggs by an inch to a rolling boil. Fill a large bowl with room-temperature water. Gently lower in 3 or 4 eggs in the boiling water and cook for 5 minutes over medium-high heat. Remove the eggs to the water bath. Repeat with the remaining eggs and take the pot off the heat.

When the eggs are cool, gently peel them, and put them back in the cooking water, which should be warm, but not hot. Leave the eggs on the back of the stove.

In the same skillet you used for the mushrooms, add the stock and let it reduce over medium-high heat until it coats the back of a spoon. Remove from the heat and stir in the butter. Swirl the skillet until the sauce looks shiny and rich. Add the mushrooms, peas, and squash runners back into the skillet and toss to coat.

If the eggs have cooled completely at this point, gently heat the water back up until the eggs are just warmed. Divide the mushroom-pea mixture into bowls, top each with an egg, a couple of slices of prosciutto, and a shave or two of lemon zest. Finish with smoked salt.

PUT AN EGG ON IT
We often joke around and say, "When in doubt, throw an egg on it." Truth is, that's one of our fail-proof cooking methods. Eggs have a way of making everything better, and they can also bring together different components of a dish. From a salad to steaks, they almost always work, whether they're soft-boiled, poached, or fried. Hot or cold, there's really no wrong they can do. So go for it, throw an egg on it.

RADISH SALAD
WITH BOTTARGA
SERVES 4

This salad takes only a couple of minutes to make, and the key is using good radishes. Go to the farmers' market, see what varieties they have, and taste them. (If the radishes bend rather than snap, they're past their prime.) Buy a nice big assortment, cut them up, then try each one with a little bit of salt and see how that completely changes the flavor. It coaxes out a little bit of the water and brings down some of the spiciness. They might be so delicious that you may decide to ditch the salad and just serve the radishes with a dish of salt.

---

16 radishes (about ¼ pound)

4 cups peppery greens, such as arugula, washed and dried (see page 255)

Grated zest and juice of ½ lemon

Extra-virgin olive oil

Salt

Bottarga or Parmesan cheese (see Note)

2 tablespoons fresh parsley

NOTE: BOTTARGA
Bottarga is cured fish roe that looks like Parmesan flakes stained an amber gold. It's got the same salty, savory characteristics as Parm but also this briny funk. If you have access to good bottarga, then definitely use it here to take the salad to the next level. It has a pretty good shelf life, and because a little goes a long way, you can get a lot of mileage out of one package. But feel free to use a good Parmesan cheese, which will also add complexity to the dish.

If you're making this salad for 4 people, think 4 different kinds of radishes for each person. Small French radishes you can just cut in half, but the other types should be thinly sliced—either with a knife or mandoline. Put them in a bowl. Add the greens to the bowl. Add the lemon juice and enough olive oil to lightly coat the lettuce, and season to taste with salt. (You'll want to err on the side of caution with the salt since bottarga and Parmesan are naturally salty.) With a Microplane, grate a couple shavings of lemon zest and a nice thin film of bottarga or Parm on top—just enough to get a little in every bite. Then top the whole thing with a handful of parsley. And that's it.

APPLE TARTE TATIN

SERVES 8

This is a slow-cooked version of the classic, with a richer, deeper, more decadent flavor. You don't need to fuss with thinly slicing the apples, and you can cook it right in your cast-iron skillet.

FOR THE FILLING

3 or 4 apples that will hold their shape after a long cooking, such as Cortland, Northern Spy, Winesap, or Rome

8 tablespoons (1 stick) unsalted butter

½ cup plus 2 tablespoons light brown sugar, lightly packed

FOR THE PASTRY

10 tablespoons (1¼ sticks) unsalted butter, softened

1⅓ cups (5.8 ounces) all-purpose flour

¼ cup plus 3 tablespoons sour cream

Pinch of granulated sugar

Crème fraîche or clotted cream, for serving

Make the filling: Peel, halve, and core the apples. Melt the butter in an 8-inch cast-iron skillet over medium-high heat, then add the brown sugar. Arrange the apples cut side down in the pan, making sure they are squeezed in tightly, since they'll shrink as they cook.

Cook until the juices from the apples bubble, then turn down to a simmer and cover the pan with a lid. Continue cooking until the apples are tender and most of the liquid in the pan has evaporated, about 30 minutes. Check peri-odically to make sure the apples don't burn. Remove from the stove, flip the apples so they are cut side up, and allow to cool completely.

Meanwhile, make the dough: Rub the soft-ened butter and flour between your thumbs and index fingers. After several minutes it will begin to incorporate into the flour. Continue until the butter is in pea-size pieces and the flour-butter mixture is fairly even in consis-tency. Stir in the sour cream until completely incorporated.

Turn out the dough onto a lightly floured work surface and knead just until smooth. Form it into a disk, cover with plastic wrap, and allow it to rest in the fridge for at least 1 hour.

Preheat the oven to 350°F. Roll out the dough on your floured work surface so it is big enough to cover the pan plus about 1 inch. Transfer the dough to the top of the pan, molding the overhanging dough to the side of the pan. Sprinkle with the granulated sugar and bake until the pastry is golden brown, about 20 minutes. Remove the tart from the oven and allow to cool until just warm.

Place a large plate over the top of the pan and quickly flip the whole thing upside down (enlisting a partner here is a good idea). Gently shake the tart from the pan, slice, and serve with crème fraîche.

DINNER 5

Classic Arugula and Parmesan Salad

———————

Slow-Roasted Duck Fat Potatoes

———————

**Rib Eye Steaks Seared, Roasted,
and Basted in Butter**

———————

Burnt Cream

WHAT TO DRINK

Crickets at Night

———————

Big French reds, such as a Syrah or Châteauneuf-du-Pape

CRICKETS AT NIGHT

MAKES 1 COCKTAIL

After spring turns to summer and summer to fall, we all sit around a fire at night out under the stars and listen to the crickets. Chirping and humming, they are nature's white noise, bringing calm and tranquility. I think this drink complements those moments with the sweet depth of honey, the bit of fiery spice, and of course, the basil, which not only adds a kick but gives the drink the green brightness of the crickets. —*Nino*

---

3 to 4 fresh basil leaves

2 teaspoons honey, dissolved in 1 teaspoon hot water

¾ ounce fresh lemon juice

2 ounces bourbon

Pinch of crushed red pepper flakes

Shake all the ingredients with 4 to 5 cubes of ice and pour into a mason jar.

CLASSIC ARUGULA
AND PARMESAN SALAD

SERVES 1 BUT MULTIPLY AS NEEDED TO FEED A CROWD

The less you do to this salad, the better it is.

---

1 tablespoon extra-virgin olive oil

Juice from 1 lemon

2 handfuls of arugula, washed and dried (see page 255)

¼ cup roughly chopped or grated Parmesan cheese

Salt (optional)

Mix the oil with two to three tablespoons of lemon juice and toss just enough of it to coat the arugula. Add the Parmesan cheese. The Parmesan usually adds enough salt to the salad, but if salt is still what you're looking for, go for it and season to taste.

SLOW-ROASTED DUCK FAT POTATOES

SERVES 4

All we're doing here is enveloping potatoes in fat and cooking them low and slow to get a buttery, creamy potato infused with the flavors of the duck fat, garlic, and herbs. Then we hit them with some heat under the broiler for a crispy finish.

Duck fat is expensive, but you can use it a few times by passing it through a strainer once you've finished and throwing it in the fridge. Or a nice way to kind of cheat is to mix duck fat with olive oil; use as much duck fat as you have, and fill in the rest with olive oil. So if you can get duck fat, awesome. But if not, we totally get it.

---

16 fingerling potatoes, new potatoes, or other waxy potatoes

Salt

1 head of garlic, halved, exposing the cloves

½ bay leaf

1 sprig fresh thyme

1 pint duck fat, or as much as you have on hand

Olive oil, as needed

Preheat the oven to 275°F.

Rinse the potatoes under cold water and dry. Halve or quarter the potatoes—you want all the pieces to be about the same size so they'll cook evenly. Place the potatoes in a roasting pan or casserole dish and season them with salt. The duck fat will consume some of the salt, so season a bit more heavily than you normally would. You can add all kinds of flavor with your aromatics. Add the garlic, bay leaf, and thyme (or other aromatics such as rosemary, pepper, toasted coriander seeds) to the pan.

Gently melt the duck fat over low heat until very warm, then pour it into the pan. Add any oil if necessary to completely submerge the potatoes. Cover the pan with foil and place in the oven. Cook until the potatoes are fork-tender or easily pierced with a cake tester, roughly 45 minutes. But check after 30 minutes to see where you're at. Once done, take the potatoes out with a slotted spoon and place them on a baking sheet. Strain the fat and save to use another time. (Store the fat in the fridge.)

Turn the oven up to broil. Cut a little piece off one of the potatoes, taste, and adjust the seasoning if necessary. Place the potatoes under the broiler to give them a quick crisp and you're done.

RIB EYE STEAKS SEARED, ROASTED, AND BASTED IN BUTTER

SERVES 4

One of our favorite things to teach people to cook is a simple steak seasoned with nothing but salt and pepper. It blows their minds that they can make a quality steak at home, and once they've mastered the skill, they can apply it to almost any other cut of meat.

We recommend dry-aged beef because the dry aging process—where the beef hangs in a cooler for weeks, causing a great deal of its moisture to evaporate and promoting the growth of natural enzymes that break down tissue—makes for a more flavorful and tender piece of meat. It's more expensive than your typical cut, but trust us; it's well worth it. That said, if you can't swing it—or if you don't like the funk of dry-aged beef—a good-quality piece of meat with lots of marbling will do just fine (see Buying Meat on page 265).

---

2 dry-aged rib eye steaks (about 1 pound each)

Grapeseed or vegetable oil

5 garlic cloves, smashed

4 bay leaves, bruised

Kosher salt and freshly ground black pepper

Unsalted butter

Coarse sea salt

Place the steaks in one layer in a casserole or other high-sided container. Slather them with oil, making sure each steak is well coated. Top them with 4 of the garlic cloves and 3 of the bay leaves. Cover with plastic wrap and store overnight in the refrigerator.

About an hour before you start cooking, take the steaks out of the fridge to come to room temperature.

Preheat the oven to 325°F.

Heat a cast-iron skillet over high heat until smoking hot. Add enough oil to generously coat the bottom of the skillet.

Just before searing, pat the meat dry with paper towels and season generously with the kosher salt all over; it should look as though you're salting a sidewalk before a snowstorm. Add a few cracks of pepper.

Tip the skillet away from you so the oil pools a bit on the opposite side and carefully place the meat in the skillet to avoid splattering yourself with hot oil. Once you've set the skillet down, use your hand to rotate the meat in the skillet to carry the sear. Keep an eye on the meat; often it will contract when it hits the heat and create a concave surface over the skillet. Using a spoon or spatula, hold the center of the meat down so that it is sears evenly. Once the meat is golden brown, turn over and repeat.

Once browned on the second side, transfer the meat to a cooling rack placed over a baking sheet. If you still have meat to cook, wipe out the skillet and repeat the searing process.

When all your meat is seared and done resting, place it on the baking sheet and put it in the oven. Allow it to roast, flipping after about 10 minutes to cook evenly. Use a cake tester to test for doneness after about 20 minutes (see page 252). We prefer rib eyes a bit closer to medium than rare so that the fat actually melts.

When your meat is done, allow it to rest in a warm place for almost half of its total cooking time.

To gently finish the meat and give it an extra dose of flavor, reheat the skillet over medium heat, add a few generous spoonfuls of butter, the remaining garlic, and remaining bay leaf. When the butter foams, add the meat back to the skillet, and carefully tip the skillet toward you and baste the steaks. Allow the steaks to rest another minute or two before slicing. Sprinkle with a pinch of sea salt and serve.

BURNT CREAM

SERVES 6

This is a classic crème brûlée, simple, rich, and sweet, and perfect after a buttery steak. And since *crème brûlée* just means "burnt cream" in French anyway, why not call it that?

---

1 cup whole milk

2¼ cups heavy cream

1 vanilla bean, split lengthwise

6 large egg yolks

1¼ cups sugar, plus extra for topping

Preheat the oven to 325°F.

Pour the milk and cream into a heavy-bottomed medium saucepan. Using the back of your knife or the side of a spoon, scrape the seeds out of the vanilla bean and add them to the pan. Bring the mixture to a simmer over low heat.

In a large heatproof mixing bowl, whisk together the egg yolks and sugar. Raise the heat on the milk-cream mixture and once it boils, pour it over the egg mixture in a thin stream, whisking constantly to combine. Pass the cream-egg mixture through a fine sieve. This is your custard base.

Divide the strained custard base into six 6-ounce ovenproof ramekins and place the dishes into a 2-inch-deep baking pan lined with dish towels, which will stop the ramekins from sliding around.

Boil a kettle of water and pour it into the baking pan so it reaches halfway up the sides of the ramekins. Bake in the oven for 30 to 40 minutes, until set. It should jiggle slightly in the middle.

Once the custards are done, remove from the baking pan and allow to cool, then place into the fridge. They can keep for up to 2 days.

To serve, top the custards with a thin layer of sugar and caramelize with a kitchen torch or under the broiler. Serve it on its own or paired with sweet fruit compote, which cuts through the richness of the custard.

WINTER

DINNER 6

Meatballs (and Spaghetti)

———

Caesar Salad with Egg in a Frame

———

Affogato with Biscotti

WHAT TO DRINK

An earthy red, such as a natural Chianti
or Montepulciano d'Abruzzo

MEATBALLS
(AND SPAGHETTI)
SERVES 8 TO 10

When it comes to meatballs, there are lots of opinions and approaches. To add to our own ideas, we dug through cookbooks and hit up our friend Ethan's mom for her motherly expertise on the subject. Sometimes moms just know best.

This dish feeds a bunch of folks, and it's also a great way to involve the hands of your friends. If you have any meatball-infused red sauce left over (meatballs leave the best mark on any red sauce), use it to make Ithai's Shakshuka (page 209) the next morning, or store it in the fridge for about 1 week, or in the freezer for about 3 months.

---

2 4- to 6-inch-long spicy or sweet sausages

4 slices of hearty bread, such as Pullman or sourdough

½ cup bread crumbs

2 pounds ground beef (ask your butcher for an 80:20 meat-to-fat ratio)

3 garlic cloves, minced

½ cup finely chopped fresh curly parsley

½ cup grated pecorino Romano

¼ cup currants

4 large eggs

2 teaspoons kosher salt

½ cup full-bodied red wine, preferably Italian

½ cup beef stock

2 generous tablespoons unsalted butter

2 quarts Red Sauce (page 204)

2 pounds spaghetti or tagliatelle

Preheat the oven to 325°F.

Pierce the sausages with a fork, then put them on a baking pan in the oven to roast, allowing their fat to caramelize them. After 20 minutes, remove the sausages from the oven and let them rest until cool enough to handle. Take the meat out of the casing and mince well.

While the sausages are cooking, add the bread and bread crumbs to a large bowl and cover with water. Soak for about a minute, then remove the mixture from the water and wring out completely. Transfer to a large clean, dry mixing bowl.

Add the minced sausages to the bowl with the bread. Toss in the beef, garlic, parsley, pecorino, currants, eggs, and salt. Mix just enough to combine. Using your hands for this puts a little more love into it, and it helps you to not overmix. Handling the meat too much can break it down, making your meatballs dense and tough. If the mixture is turning gooey, it's a sign that it is getting overworked. The mixture should be moist but not wet.

Again using your hands, shape the meatballs so they are slightly bigger than a golf ball—about the size that fits perfectly into the palm of your hand. Place them evenly spaced on a wire rack set on a rimmed baking sheet. Pour the wine and stock over the meatballs, making a shallow bath in the pan. Cover with aluminum foil and bake until the meatballs are cooked to about medium, roughly 45 minutes. They should feel firm but still yield a little when pressed.

Remove the meatballs from the pan and let them cool for 10 minutes. Now *arroser* the meatballs (see page 251). Melt the butter in a large heavy-bottomed pan over medium heat and once foaming, add as many meatballs as will comfortably fit in the pan without touching one another. Baste the meatballs continuously for about a minute. (You might find it easiest to do this in batches.)

Transfer them from the pan back to the wire rack.

Heat the red sauce in a pot large enough to accommodate the meatballs. Add the meatballs and simmer for about 20 minutes, allowing them to soak up the sauce.

Bring a large pot of water to a boil, add a handful of salt, then cook the pasta until al dente. Strain and serve with 2 meatballs per person and plenty of sauce on top. Enjoy thoroughly.

CAESAR SALAD
WITH EGG IN A FRAME
SERVES 8

This is a great twist on a pretty straightforward dish. Instead of adding croutons to the salad, we top the whole thing with a runny fried egg in a crisp slice of bread.

You'll most likely end up with more dressing than you'll need for one go-round, but it will keep in the fridge for up to 1 week.

---

2 large eggs plus 1 large yolk

Juice of 1 lemon

2 tablespoons good Dijon mustard

8 to 12 dashes of Worcestershire sauce

2 garlic cloves

½ white onion, roughly chopped

4 to 6 anchovy fillets

About 3 cups extra-virgin olive oil

Salt and freshly ground black pepper

4 to 6 heads of baby romaine lettuce, washed and dried (see page 255)

2 shallots, thinly sliced

8 Eggs in a Frame (recipe follows)

Freshly grated pecorino Romano

2 tablespoons chopped fresh parsley

First, make the dressing. In the bowl of a food processor or blender, combine the eggs and yolk, lemon juice, mustard, Worcestershire sauce, garlic, onion, and anchovies. Blend to combine, then, with the motor running, very slowly stream in the olive oil until the dressing reaches the consistency you like. We typically leave ours pretty loose. Season with salt and pepper. If you want it brighter, add more lemon juice; if you want more tang, add another dash or two of Worcestershire sauce. Adjust with salt and pepper, if necessary, or process in more oil if you like it richer or less tart.

To assemble the salad, rip the leaves into bite-size pieces.

Toss the lettuce in a bowl with the shallots and a good pinch of salt and pepper. Add just enough dressing to delicately coat the lettuce. Using your hands to mix everything together is a great way to gauge how well dressed your salad is. You want the leaves to have an even, very slight oily feel. Portion out onto individual plates or bowls and top each serving with an Egg in a Frame. Make sure they are fresh out of the skillet so the warm egg yolk can break onto the salad. Finish the whole thing off with some grated pecorino and parsley.

EGG IN A FRAME

SERVES 8

Whether you know it as Egg in a Frame, One-Eyed Susie, Toad in the Hole, or Gas House, we've all had some version of this breakfast staple as kids. It's really just bread, butter, and eggs, and yet it's insanely delicious—on its own and on top of a salad, after a long night, or when you need to feed a hungry crowd fast.

For extra credit, you can sprinkle some grated cheese over the top—sharp cheddar, Swiss, pecorino, whatever you like. If you have a few chives or another kind of fresh green herb like parsley or chervil on hand, go ahead and chop it finely and scatter it over the top.

---

8 slices Pullman or any white bread

8 tablespoons (1 stick) unsalted butter

8 large eggs

Salt and freshly ground black pepper

Grated pecorino Romano, Swiss, or sharp cheddar (optional)

Fresh herbs, such as chives, parsley, or chervil, finely chopped (optional)

GRILLED CAESAR SALAD
Grilling the lettuce is a nice way to change up a traditional Caesar for a cookout or warm summer night spent eating outside. The char adds a complex flavor to the salad, and the combination of the tender, charred leaves and the crisp raw ones is surprising and delicious. Just cut the romaine hearts in half, rub them with a little grapeseed oil, and grill them until lightly blackened. Allow them to cool before assembling the salad.

Use the rim of a small juice glass or mason jar to cut a hole in the middle of each piece of bread. Keep the small round of bread for another use.

In a large cast-iron skillet or heavy-bottomed sauté pan over medium heat, melt 1 tablespoon butter for each piece of bread that will fit in the skillet. Add as many slices of bread as will fit comfortably. Give each piece a quick flip initially to coat both sides with butter, then let them get golden brown on one side. Flip the toast, crack an egg in the middle, and season with salt and pepper. Throw a cover over the skillet, and by the time the other side is golden brown, the egg should be done. If desired, sprinkle some pecorino and herbs on top before serving.

AFFOGATO WITH BISCOTTI

SERVES 8

Affogato—or "ice cream drowned with espresso"—is beyond simple to make. To take it to the next level, try making your own orange and sweet wine–flavored ice cream. The recipe here is technically for a parfait—or a frozen dessert that's not churned—but we don't think your guests will mind.

FOR THE ICE CREAM

1½ cups granulated sugar

1 cup sweet dessert wine (your favorite affordable one)

1 cup orange juice, strained

9 large eggs, separated

Seeds of 2 vanilla beans

3 cups heavy cream

¾ cup powdered sugar

FOR SERVING

½ cup unsalted pistachios (enough to scatter on each bowl), toasted (see page 255)

8 biscotti

8 shots espresso or amaretto

Set up a double boiler by half-filling a large saucepan with water. Bring it to a simmer over medium heat. Place a medium metal bowl on top of the saucepan, but don't let it touch the water. (You can pour out water until it fits.)

Add ¾ cup of the granulated sugar, wine, orange juice, egg yolks, and vanilla-bean seeds to the bowl and whisk until the mixture is thick enough to hold figure eights. Take the bowl off the saucepan and continue whisking until the mixture cools.

In an electric mixer with the whisk attachment, whisk together the cream and powdered sugar just until soft peaks form. (Or do this by hand.) Remove the whipped cream to a large, clean bowl and carefully wash out and dry the mixer bowl.

In the electric mixer, whisk the egg whites until soft peaks form, then gently stir in the remaining ¾ cup granulated sugar. Don't overmix or you'll lose all the air from the egg whites.

Fold the cooked yolk mixture into the whipped cream, then gently fold that mixture into the egg whites.

Transfer the ice-cream base to containers and freeze overnight.

Once frozen completely, it's ready to serve. Simply put a scoop of ice cream in each bowl or dessert cup, add a generous pinch of pistachios and a biscotti, and top with freshly pulled espresso.

DINNER 7

Duck Confit and Tagliatelle

**Radicchio Salad with Pears,
Bleu Cheese, and Bacon**

WHAT TO DRINK

Smoked Earl Grey Hot Toddy

A light- to medium-bodied red,
such as a light Burgundy or Pinot Noir

SMOKED EARL GREY HOT TODDY

MAKES 1 COCKTAIL

Adding an aromatic tea to a hot toddy gives it an extra dimension of warmth and complexity. If you can get smoked Earl Grey, the effect is insane, but regular Earl Grey is great as well. Adding a small taste of an amaro like Averna goes really well here and adds a bit of depth to the drink. —*Nino*

1 heaping tablespoon honey

2 to 3 lemon slices

5 whole cloves

1 cinnamon stick

1 cup smoked Earl Grey tea (still hot)

2 ounces brandy, rye, or bourbon

¼ ounce amaro, such as Averna (optional)

Warm a mug by filling it with boiling water and letting it sit for a few minutes. Pour out the water. To the bottom of the mug, add the honey, lemons, cloves, and cinnamon. Pour in the hot tea, stir until the honey is fully dissolved, then pour in the brandy and the amaro (if using). Continue stirring until it is the right temperature for you. Best served in front of a fire or while fresh snow is falling.

DUCK CONFIT AND TAGLIATELLE

SERVES 4

This dish is about embracing the earthy textures of winter that make you feel warm-bellied and satisfied. As we worked to perfect this dish, we kept in mind how we could bring together heavier flavors without making you want to fall asleep on the couch after eating. The walnut Marsala sauce lends the rich duck a lightness and acidity that makes this whole dish sit nice and easy in the stomach.

Grapeseed or vegetable oil

1 medium shallot, diced small

Salt

1 small garlic clove, grated

1 cup Marsala or Madeira

2 cups duck or beef stock

2 legs Duck Confit (recipe follows)

½ cup crushed walnuts

2 generous tablespoons unsalted butter

8 2-inch-long sunchokes, cut into ¼-inch slices

1 lemon, cut into wedges

Coarse sea salt (optional)

1 pound tagliatelle

1 cup grated Parmesan cheese

¼ cup chopped fresh parsley

Preheat the oven to 400°F.

In a medium saucepan or saucier pan over low heat, warm enough oil to cover the bottom, then sweat down the shallot until translucent, about 5 minutes. Once sweet-smelling and softened, lightly season with salt, then add the garlic. Sweat for another minute, then get ready to pour the Marsala into your pan. If you're using a gas stove, keep in mind that you're about to add a lot of booze to a pan over an open flame. You'll want to carefully pour it in off the flame to avoid it catching on fire / burning you / burning down your kitchen. (If it does catch fire, not to worry, just turn off your burner and simply allow the flames to burn off all the alcohol.)

Bring the Marsala to a boil over medium heat, then reduce to a simmer. Cook until it begins to thicken enough to coat the back of a spoon, about 3 minutes. Add your stock and repeat the reduction process.

Once your sauce has reduced to the point where it now looks a bit thinner than maple syrup, remove the pan from the heat and let it hang out on the back of the stove. You want the sauce to be on the looser side now because eventually you'll heat it back up to incorporate the pasta and it will reduce further as it coats the noodles. If you reduce it too much at first, your pasta will be pasty. If this happens, add a touch more of the pasta's cooking water to the sauce.

(recipe continues)

Using your fingers, tear up the duck confit into bite-size pieces. Add this and the crushed walnuts to your sauce and reserve.

Warm 1 of the tablespoons of butter in a large cast-iron skillet over medium heat and allow it to foam and lightly brown. Throw in the sunchokes and a pinch of salt. Cook until they have taken on a bit of color and softened but still have a little crunch, 5 to 6 minutes. Take care not to let the butter burn. Once the sunchokes are done, transfer them to a small bowl. Finish them by squeezing over a little lemon juice to brighten their flavor, adding some coarse sea salt too, if needed. Set them aside.

Cook your tagliatelle in boiling, salted water until al dente. Strain, reserving about ½ cup of the pasta's cooking water; add the water to your sauce. Warm the sauce over low heat, add the remaining tablespoon of butter, and stir as it heats to make sure the butter emulsifies nicely. Taste for seasoning, then add your pasta to the pan. Give it a quick toss, add the sunchokes, throw in a solid handful of grated Parmesan, and finish with parsley.

PASTA WATER: AN UNDERRATED INGREDIENT

It's a classic Italian grandmother's secret to reserve some of the pasta cooking water to give sauce a little more body. The same principle works for any pasta dish that's on the dry side. A little bit of starchy water tossed in at the end of the cooking process can also bring a dish together, from binding sauces together to helping sauce coat the pasta. Simply add the water little by little until your desired consistency is achieved.

DUCK CONFIT

MAKES 2 DUCK LEGS

Confit is just a fussy way of saying "something slow-cooked in fat." This is a slow, smooth little dance to render out the duck's fat and infuse the meat with the flavor of thyme and garlic until it's falling off the bone. And once you're done, it's the dish that keeps on giving. Just strain all that flavorful duck fat and store it in the fridge so that you can use it another time to fry up some potatoes. Traditionally, duck confit is cured first, but since we're going for simple, we're skipping that step.

We recommend making more than you need at one time. If you double the recipe, you'll have leftovers to make sandwiches the next day.

---

2 duck legs

Salt

2 quarts duck fat or as much as you can get and supplement with olive oil (see Note)

4 sprigs fresh thyme

¼ head of garlic

1 bay leaf

Small handful of whole black peppercorns

NOTE: DUCK FAT
If you have duck fat, then by all means, do this in duck fat. Chances are, though, that you're not always going to be able to get it or enough of it. If you can scrounge up a small tub, add some olive oil to get the amount you need. Or you can use all olive oil if duck fat isn't a reality.

Preheat the oven to 225°F.

In a shallow-sided sauté pan, season the duck legs all over with salt and cover completely with the duck fat so they are fully submerged. If your duck fat is congealed solid when it comes out of the fridge, heat it gently in a pan to melt it before adding to the legs. Add the thyme, garlic, bay leaf, and peppercorns.

Loosely cover the pan with foil and throw in the oven. Let it ride until the meat is falling-off-the-bone tender, 2½ to 3 hours. Remove and let cool.

Pull the meat off the bone and use now, or if you want to save some of the duck for another time, just strain the fat while still warm enough (not hot!) to pour through a sieve to remove the aromatics, then store the duck submerged in the fat in the fridge. It will keep for at least a few months that way. When you're ready to serve, reheat it as slowly and at as low a temperature as possible to avoid cooking the duck further.

RADICCHIO SALAD
WITH PEARS, BLEU CHEESE, AND BACON
SERVES 4

Pear, bleu cheese, and bacon are a classic flavor combination. Using the drippings rendered from the bacon to make a vinaigrette and adding bitter radicchio and almost-sweet celery root elevates this salad to makes this a much smokier, brighter, more elevated affair.

---

1 thick slice of smoky, fatty bacon

1 head of radicchio

Extra-virgin olive oil

Champagne vinegar

2 teaspoons Dijon mustard

½ garlic clove, grated

Salt and freshly ground black pepper

2 Seckel pears

1 small celery root

1 cup roughly chopped nuts, such as pistachios, walnuts, or pecans

½ cup crumbled good-quality, tangy bleu cheese or any other salty, funky cheese

Finely chopped fresh mixed herbs, such as parsley, chervil, chives, and mint

Slice the bacon crosswise to make ¼-inch-thick lardons.

In a small cast-iron skillet or heavy-bottomed sauté pan over low heat, slowly cook the bacon. The idea is to render as much fat as possible, which will make for a tastier vinaigrette and crispier bacon. When crisp, transfer the lardons to a paper-towel-lined plate and pour the drippings into a small mason jar. Let cool.

Halve the head of radicchio, cut out the tough inner core, and tear the leaves into bite-size pieces. You only need to prep about a big handful per person. The rest can be stored in the fridge for later salads. Clean and dry the leaves you're using and transfer to a big bowl.

Add enough olive oil to the bacon fat so there are equal parts bacon fat and oil. This will keep the dressing from getting too heavy and help the renderings stretch a little further.

Pour in the champagne vinegar, enough to double the amount of oil. Add the mustard and garlic, then give the dressing a shake at this point and taste—it should be bright but not burn the back of your throat, and it shouldn't taste too heavy and oily. Adjust the oil/vinegar ratio if necessary and season to taste with salt and pepper. Salt will help bring out the flavor and brightness in the vinegar. Give the mason jar another shake, taste again, and adjust the seasoning again, if necessary.

Cut the "cheeks" or meaty sides off the pears and slice. Add to the bowl with the lettuce.

Cut the knobby root end off the celery root and peel the skin using either a peeler or by running your knife down the sides. Halve the celery root and slice half of it paper thin with your knife or a mandoline. You'll want to do this close to the time you're serving because the flesh will start to oxidize and turn brown. Add it to the mixture in the bowl.

Throw in the nuts, bleu cheese, lardons, and herbs, then season the whole lot with salt and pepper—just remember that the bacon and bleu cheese will be salty, too. Toss it all together with your hands before adding the dressing. It will mix much more easily and evenly that way.

Be slow with the vinaigrette at first; you don't want a wet salad. Pour a little in at a time and mix using your hands until everything is well coated.

A NOTE ON VINAIGRETTE

Traditional French vinaigrettes call for one part vinegar to three parts oil. It's an old-school method and it makes a vinaigrette taste more like oil than anything else. We'll probably catch flack from a purist French chef, but we believe a vinaigrette should bring flavors forward using acidity as opposed to covering them up with oil, so we use more vinegar.

Most of the vinaigrettes in this book aren't Escoffier-approved anyhow, as we don't always fully emulsify the oil and vinegar. The quick-and-easy way to make a dressing instead is to put the ingredients in a mason jar and give it shake. This is also helpful because you can see the vinegar-to-oil ratio as the layers settle. It's a little imperfect and a little broken, but it works.

ON COFFEE

JERAD MORRISON AND JUSTIN MORRISON
Sightglass Coffee

Walking into Sightglass Coffee, Jerad and Justin Morrison's San Francisco coffee shop, I thought I was in for a long-winded philosophy about beans and brewing. But it turns out that the brothers approach coffee not with a sense of holiness, but rather with the understanding that good (fair trade) product and technique go a long way. They're just two guys who enjoy a quality cup of coffee and want to help people make theirs a little better at home.

We started Sightglass in 2009. Our goal was straightforward: to make delicious coffee through thoughtful sourcing, roasting, and preparation. Coffee is our craft. To us, a good craftsperson works tirelessly to perfect and deliver excellence. We want this idea to take root in our cafes, but we also want to help people make great coffee at home.

Making delicious coffee can be a simple and rewarding endeavor, and the recipes call for minimal supplies, steps, and ingredients. Because they are so simple, it is most important that you choose a great coffee, store it properly, and make it well.

| CHOOSING A COFFEE |

When possible, look for coffees that are whole bean, roasted locally, and are sourced responsibly. Whole beans keep their freshness and fragrance longer than grounds. The sooner you use coffee after it has been ground, the better it'll taste. As for who to buy coffee from, it's just like going to the farmers' market for produce—supporting local business puts a premium on transparency. There are a lot of politics in the coffee market, so finding a company that takes pride in where they're sourcing from and supports fair trade is one way to make sure that you can feel good about where you're spending your money.

The flavor in coffee is incredibly complex, and it's amazing how much it can differ from country to country, farm to farm, even batch to batch. But in general, you can look for general characteristics that are common to regions.

In terms of flavor, if you like . . .

FLORAL: Try coffees from Colombia.

FRUITY: Try coffees from Africa.

CHOCOLATE: Try coffees from Guatemala.

In terms of body, if you like . . .

SYRUPY: Try coffees that are blends.

DELICATE: Try coffees from Central America.

HEAVY: Try an espresso roast.

| STORING COFFEE |

Store your coffee in a cool, dark place, preferably in an airtight container. Never put coffee in the refrigerator, as it can absorb off-flavors, and cold coffee beans won't brew properly. However, if you're not going to use the coffee for an extended period of time, you can store it in an airtight container in the freezer, letting it come back to room temperature before brewing. Otherwise, enjoy your coffee within 2 to 3 weeks of the printed roast date. Coffee behaves a lot like a helium balloon—after a few weeks, the flavor and intensity will deflate.

| BREWING COFFEE |

Chemex is our brew method of choice for the home. Originally invented in 1941 by a chemist, this pour-over coffee brewer is made of glass with a wooden handle. It uses a thicker filter than most, which produces an aromatic, clean, and syrupy cup.

This recipe makes two 10-ounce mugs of coffee, enough to share. We have also included an iced version of this recipe that can be shared among friends on an easygoing morning. Enjoy!

POUR-OVER COFFEE

SERVES 2 TO 4

3½ cups water, preferably filtered

½ cup whole-bean coffee

SPECIAL EQUIPMENT

narrow-spouted kettle; coffee grinder, ideally with burrs, not blades; white Chemex filter (brown Chemex filters have a bit more of a paper-forward flavor and will require an extra rinse); 6-cup Chemex

Pour the water in the kettle and bring to a boil. Meanwhile, grind the beans (if your grinder doesn't have recommended settings for pour-over, grind it so that it resembles something like fine demerara sugar or kosher salt, halfway between the fineness for espresso and for a drip machine).

Place the filter into the Chemex and rinse it with tap water. Discard the rinse water and place the coffee grounds in the filter.

Once the water reaches a boil, remove from the stove and set aside for 30 seconds.

Pour the water over the coffee to bloom, stopping just when all of the grounds have been saturated (about ½ cup of water). If your coffee is fresh, you will see a little bit of froth. This is the coffee releasing its carbon dioxide; waiting here for a moment allows for even extraction. Wait 45 seconds to 1 minute, or until the color of the coffee goes from caramel brown to fudge brown.

Slowly pour the remaining water over the coffee in small concentric circles, taking care to not pour directly onto the filter. Pause if the water reaches 1 inch below the Chemex rim. This will help ensure that you pull all the flavor and strength from the ground coffee. Let the water level begin to drop about ½ inch, then pour again. Continue until all of the water has been poured. This should take around 4 minutes. Pour into mugs and enjoy.

ICED COFFEE

SERVES 2 TO 4

2 cups water, preferably filtered

½ cup whole-bean coffee

SPECIAL EQUIPMENT

narrow-spouted kettle; coffee grinder, ideally with burrs, not blades; white Chemex filter; 6-cup Chemex

Follow the instructions as for Pour-Over Coffee, left, but when you pour the boiling water in the Chemex, stop 2 inches below the rim. Let the water level drop about ¼ inch, then pour again. Continue until all of the water has been poured. This should take about 3 minutes.

Fill a 16-ounce heatproof glass with cubed ice. We recommend using larger square ice cubes, but any ice will work. Pour the hot coffee over the ice to fill half of the glass; since the coffee is concentrated, it will be diluted to the proper strength with the melted ice. Swirl until cold and enjoy.

DINNER 8

Chris's Roasted Lamb Shoulder

———

Rutabaga Puree

———

Anchovy Watercress Salad

———

Treacle Tart

WHAT TO DRINK

Syrah and other earthy reds from Languedoc
or German Blaufränkisch, because of its
dark forest fruit characteristics

CHRIS'S ROASTED LAMB SHOULDER

SERVES 8

A few years ago, I was lucky enough to stage (or intern) at the London restaurant St. John Bread and Wine while the epically talented James Lowe was head chef. One of the best tricks James taught me was how to patiently slow-roast a piece of meat at a low temperature in order to gradually soften it and ensure a nice and tender texture. This method is perfect for lamb shoulder because you can keep the meat juicy and rare—a rich and rewarding end. It's a cut of meat that can be a bit pricey, but a 4-pound roast goes a long way since you only need a little to feel satisfied.

The recipes in this menu are inspired by what I learned at St. John. It's my homage to James for all the amazing techniques and know-how he was so generous to share.

---

3 sprigs fresh rosemary

1 bay leaf

2 garlic cloves, smashed

2 anchovies (optional, but delicious)

1 boneless lamb shoulder (about 4 pounds)

Salt

Grapeseed or vegetable oil

1 cup Sauvignon Blanc or other dry white wine

Coarse sea salt

Preheat the oven to 250°F.

Tuck 2 sprigs of the rosemary, the bay leaf, garlic, and anchovies (if using) into where the lamb shoulder has been deboned. Starting at one end, truss the lamb by tying it up with kitchen twine at 2-inch intervals or so until you get to the other end. Four or five loops should work; don't overdo it. Then, using the tip of your knife, make small incisions all around the surface of the lamb. Cut the remaining sprig of rosemary into 1-inch-long segments and stuff them into the holes. Salt the lamb all over.

Over a medium-high flame, heat a large cast-iron skillet and coat the bottom with oil. When the oil is shimmering-hot, place the shoulder in the skillet and let sear on all four sides until a beautiful brown color. Remove the lamb from the skillet and place it on a rimmed baking sheet or roasting pan lightly greased with oil. Pour the wine over the top and put the dish in the oven. Roast until the cake tester feels warm (not hot) to your lip (see page 252). If double-checking with a thermometer, you're looking for 130°F for rare, 135°F for medium-rare. Begin checking on the roast after about 1 hour in the oven.

Once it's finished, let the lamb rest on a wire rack for 10 minutes. Then cut the string and remove the herbs and anchovies from inside the roast, if desired. Cut the roast crosswise into ¾-inch-thick slices, finish with sea salt, and serve.

RUTABAGA PUREE

SERVES 6 TO 8

This is one of the most simple, yet rewarding, dishes I learned during my time at St. John. It falls right in line with the restaurant's ethos: Although simple, if these two roots from the ground are treated just right, the dish can please just about anyone. All you have to remember is equal parts yellow or sweet onion to rutabaga and never to let the onions brown—just sweeten them by sweating them gently until translucent.

You'll end up with quite a bit of puree, so you can stash it in the fridge and use it to pair with any roasted meat, or even with a hearty grain like quinoa. Pretty much wherever you might serve something with mashed potatoes, this puree will work.

Grapeseed or vegetable oil

1½ pounds yellow or sweet onions (about 3 medium onions), diced small (no need to be too picky about how uniform the pieces are since they'll ultimately be pureed)

1½ pounds rutabaga (about 1 big one)

Salt

1½ sprigs fresh rosemary and/or a few fresh sage leaves, chopped

12 tablespoons (1½ sticks) unsalted butter, or as needed

Coarse sea salt

Over a medium-low flame, heat a large stockpot with enough oil to generously coat the bottom. When the oil is just barely shimmering, add the onions. Here's where you really have to pay attention to make sure you won't cook the onions too quickly and brown them. The sizzle you hear when the onions hit the oil should be gentle, not ecstatic. No onion pieces should stick to the bottom of the pot or turn even slightly brown.

Reduce the heat to low, and cover the pot but leave the lid slightly ajar. Keep an eye on the onions and stir every few minutes, making sure they're cooking at the perfect "sweating temperature." You can add more oil if the onions aren't completely coated. Continue to let them cook until they are soft and sweet-smelling, about 10 minutes.

As the onions sweat, peel and roughly cut the rutabaga to ¾-inch cubes (again, no need to go crazy over the size; it is going to get blended up). When the onions are done, add a pinch of salt and a touch more oil, stir, then add the rutabaga and herbs. Season with salt, and let the onion-rutabaga mixture continue to sweat at a gentle temperature until the rutabaga feels soft and is easily pierced with a cake tester.

At this point, add enough butter to coat the vegetables. This is comfort food, so add more or less depending on your preference. Then transfer the mixture to a blender or food processor and process until smooth. Blend in more butter if desired, and season to taste with sea salt.

ANCHOVY WATERCRESS SALAD

SERVES 8

Anchovies are the secret weapon in many chefs' arsenals. They act as a flavor-deepening element, sort of like a mushroom or salt. This recipe uses them in the vinaigrette, but you could also toss a couple of fillets in the pan when you *arroser* meat (see page 251). They'll dissolve right into the hot butter. You'll want to go for high-quality anchovies in moderation to get this effect. If you skimp on quality, your dish will just taste fishy.

The peppery flavor of watercress balanced with this bright vinaigrette make a great complement to the richness of the lamb and the earthiness of the pureed rutabaga. If you can't find watercress, though, you could use another bitter or spicy salad green in its place, such as radicchio or arugula.

Juice of 3 lemons, reserving zest of 1 lemon for garnish

¼ cup olive oil

2 teaspoons Dijon mustard

Freshly ground black pepper, to taste

6 to 10 anchovies, finely chopped

2 bunches of watercress, washed and dried (see page 255)

4 shallots, sliced into very thin rings

Make the dressing by mixing together the lemon juice, oil, mustard, black pepper, and anchovies. Use your hands to toss as much dressing as desired with the watercress. (The rest keeps in a jar in the fridge for 5 days.) Place a handful of greens on each plate, top with a few shallot rings, and garnish with a pinch of grated lemon zest.

TREACLE TART

SERVES 12

Treacle tart is a delicious traditional English dessert, keeping with the British menu we have here. It is dense and sweet and rich, and a little goes a long way. Treacle tart is usually made with golden syrup, which is similar to molasses, only with a cleaner sweetness. Since golden syrup—like treacle tart—is very British, it's worth trying to track some down. Plus, you can always use the leftovers for pancakes. But if you can't find golden syrup, cane syrup or even light molasses will do just fine.

FOR THE PASTRY CRUST

7 tablespoons unsalted butter, softened, plus extra for greasing the pan

6 tablespoons (2.5 ounces) sugar

3 large egg yolks

1⅔ cups (7 ounces) all-purpose flour, plus extra for dusting

FOR THE FILLING

14 tablespoons (1¾ sticks) unsalted butter

4 cups golden syrup or cane syrup or light molasses

3 large eggs

¼ cup plus 1 tablespoon heavy cream

2 teaspoons salt

Zest of 3 lemons

Juice of 2 lemons

2 cups bread crumbs, ideally made from the crust of soft white bread (don't use a heavy loaf or the flavor will be too strong and the texture too dense)

Vanilla ice cream, for serving

SPECIAL EQUIPMENT

8-inch tart pan with removable bottom; pie weights or 1 16-ounce bag dried beans

Mix the pastry dough: In a large bowl, cream the butter and sugar together until well combined, then beat in the egg yolks, one at a time, until fully incorporated into the mixture. Stir in the flour until the mixture comes together as a ball of dough. Scoop out the dough onto a floured work surface and knead briefly, just until smooth.

Wrap the pastry in plastic wrap and chill in the refrigerator for 30 minutes.

Make the filling: In a small saucepan, melt the butter over medium heat until it smells nutty and the milk solids have separated and browned. Be careful not to burn. Set aside.

In another small saucepan, gently warm the golden syrup over low heat so that it loosens up but doesn't get hot. Set aside.

In a large bowl, combine the eggs, cream, and salt, then add the warmed golden syrup and butter, plus the lemon zest and lemon juice. Stir in the crumbs, which will soak up all the liquid.

Roll and blind-bake the tart shell: Grease the tart pan with softened butter. Dust the pan lightly with flour, tapping out any excess.

On a floured work surface, roll out the dough to a 9- or 10-inch round. Fit the dough into the tart pan, making sure there's an inch or two extra hanging over the side. Refrigerate for 20 more minutes.

Preheat the oven to 350°F.

Remove the now-rested pastry dough from the fridge and trim away any excess that hangs over the side of the pan. Punch holes all over the dough with a fork to keep it from rising in the oven. Line the top of the dough with parchment paper, then top with pie weights to fill the tart pan. This will keep the dough from puffing up as it bakes. Put the tart shell into the oven and bake until the bottom is cooked and slightly golden, about 20 minutes. Remove the pie weights and parchment paper and finish cooking until the pastry is golden brown, about 5 minutes. Remove from the oven and leave to cool.

Fill and finish the tart: Lower the oven to 300°F. Pour the filling mixture into the cooked tart shell and bake for 50 minutes, or until it is set in the center and cracks appear at the edges. Let cool, and serve with vanilla ice cream.

DINNER 9

White Bean Spread on Toast

Spicy Tomato Stew with Seared Halibut

WHAT TO DRINK

Kings County Sour

A light and fresh white wine,
such as a dry Prosecco or Pinot Gris

KINGS COUNTY SOUR

MAKES 1 COCKTAIL

I had to give a nod to my place of birth: Brooklyn! This is a play on a classic New York sour but uses rye instead of bourbon for a bit more spice and port wine instead of red table wine for a touch more depth—just like Brooklyn itself. —*Nino*

½ ounce simple syrup (see page 61)

¾ ounce freshly squeezed lemon juice

1 egg white

2 ounces rye whiskey

Splash of club soda

Splash of port wine

Orange twist

Brandied cherry

Shake together the simple syrup, lemon juice, egg white, and rye with ice. Strain into a chilled old-fashioned glass. Top with a splash of club soda and float the port on top. Garnish with an orange twist and brandied cherry.

WHITE BEAN SPREAD ON TOAST

SERVES 4 TO 6

Since we're already soaking some beans for the Spicy Tomato Stew with Seared Halibut (opposite), we thought we might as well soak some more to make an olive-oil-rich bean spread, which goes well with pretty much everything from sandwiches and eggs to meat and fish. Or, of course, toast. (Thin out the puree with some stock for a smoother consistency that's better suited for delicate proteins.) You can go simple with just olive oil, salt, and pepper, or throw in any aromatics you have lying around. Garlic, rosemary, bay leaf, even bacon—it all works. Use them to flavor the beans as they cook and/or punch things up at the end with a palmful of fresh herbs or, our favorite, a few cloves of roasted garlic.

---

1 cup dried flageolet or white beans

Extra-virgin olive oil

1 tablespoon chopped fresh rosemary or other herbs (optional)

A few cloves of roasted garlic (optional)

Salt and freshly ground black pepper

1 baguette, sliced and toasted

The night or two before cooking, soak the beans in water, covering them by a few inches. Set them in the fridge. This softens them up and reduces their cooking time. When you're ready to cook, strain the beans, discarding the water.

Generally speaking, the ratio of water to pre-soaked beans is 3:1. Add the beans and 3 cups unsalted water to a large saucepan. Add a tablespoon of oil and any herbs you want to use.

Bring the water to a boil over high heat, and then reduce to a simmer. Cook for about 45 minutes, or until the beans are still holding their shape but are creamy inside. Once done, strain the beans (reserving the liquid) and place them in a food processor or blender. Add about ¼ cup of the cooking liquid and process while slowly adding oil until you reach the consistency you're looking for (ideally a thick puree). You could also do this with just cooking water.

When the spread is thick and smooth, finish it off, if desired, with any aromatics you have a taste for—a palmful of chopped rosemary or a few cloves of roasted garlic. Season with salt and pepper to taste. Slather it on toast and serve.

SPICY TOMATO STEW
WITH SEARED HALIBUT

SERVES 4

If you already have a bunch of our Red Sauce (page 204) stocked in your freezer, this dish just got that much easier to make. If not, buy some good red sauce at the market. The key word is *good* because the better the red sauce, the better the dish. With a quality (already-seasoned) sauce as the base of this stew, you don't have to do much besides add creamy beans, seared fish, and a crusty loaf of bread for a meal in a bowl.

Grapeseed or vegetable oil

Crushed red pepper flakes

4 cups Red Sauce (page 204)

2 cups chicken or vegetable stock

¼ cup dried flageolet or white beans, soaked in water overnight

3 ounces any good-quality dried charcuterie sausage, cut into small bite-size pieces

1 shallot, thinly sliced (optional)

½ pound kale, stripped from the ribs and torn into bite-size pieces, washed and dried (see page 255)

Salt

4 halibut, mahi mahi, or cod fillets (4 to 6 ounces each) from the middle of the fish (tail pieces go from thick to thin pretty dramatically and are harder to cook evenly)

Wondra flour

4 generous tablespoons unsalted butter, cut into chunks

3 tablespoons finely chopped fresh cilantro

Coat the bottom of a large deep sauté pan with oil and heat over a medium-low flame. Add 1 to 1½ tablespoons red pepper flakes and gently heat to infuse the oil with the flavor.

Add the red sauce, stock, and strained beans. Bring the pot to a boil over medium-high heat, then turn it back down to a simmer. Allow the contents to cook gently while reducing to a thick stewlike consistency. If the stew starts getting thick and the beans aren't tender, add more stock or water and continue to simmer. You can repeat this process until the beans are cooked, but make sure if you're adding more than one go-round of stock that you're also adding a bit more sauce to balance the flavor. This will take from 25 to 45 minutes, depending on your beans.

Once the beans are cooked and the mixture is thick, add the sausage and cook another minute or two to incorporate the flavor.

At this point, let your stew hang out, covered, on the back of your range over very low heat while you finish the dish. Generously coat

(recipe continues)

the bottom of a large cast-iron skillet with oil and heat over a medium-high flame. Add the shallot and fry until golden. Remove from the skillet and let it drain on a paper-towel-lined plate. Add the kale to the skillet with a pinch of salt and quickly sauté until softened. Set aside.

Dust the fish on both sides with the Wondra flour.

Wipe out the pan and set over medium-high heat with enough oil to coat the bottom. When the oil is shimmering hot, carefully add the fillets to the pan, and salt them. Turn down the heat if they are sizzling like crazy; you want them to be lively, but not screaming.

When you see a golden crust form on the bottom of the fish, add the butter to the pan and let it foam and steam the fish a bit. Carefully flip the fillets and lightly salt them. Then gently tip the pan toward you, and using a spoon, baste the fillets with that hot butter for a minute or two. Use a cake tester to check the doneness of the fish—you want it to slide in easily, with almost no resistance, or go ahead and cut into a piece if you're not sure. When the fish is just barely translucent, you're ready. Remove the fish to a warm plate lined with paper towels and let it rest for a minute.

Once the fish is done, divide the stew into bowls, topped with a piece of fish, shallots and kale, and a generous pinch of cilantro.

DINNER 10

Pork Chops and Charred Applesauce

Braised Fennel with Mint

Roasted New Potatoes

Lillie's Sticky Toffee Pudding

WHAT TO DRINK

A light and slightly juicy red,
such as Pinot Noir or Cabernet Franc

PORK CHOPS
AND CHARRED APPLESAUCE

SERVES 4

Pork chops have a bad rap as bone-dry hunks of pale, sad-looking protein. But when cooked right, they are flavorful and golden and tender. If you want, you can brine the pork chops first, which makes them extra juicy. It's an added step that's definitely worth your time, but even if you don't, you're already ahead of the game just by following our meat-searing method (see page 253).

¼ cup kosher salt

2 1½-inch-thick pork chops, preferably double bone-in, which you can request at the butcher

Grapeseed oil

4 tablespoons (½ stick) unsalted butter

Leaves from 1 sprig fresh rosemary or a few fresh sage leaves, chopped fine (optional)

Coarse sea salt

1 pint Charred Applesauce (recipe follows)

Make the brine by combining the kosher salt with 4 cups of water in a large plastic zipper-lock bag or a bowl big enough so the chops can be fully submerged. Place the chops into the brine and refrigerate for 30 minutes, or up to 6 hours. Remove the chops from the brine, rinse, and pat very dry. Discard the brine.

Preheat the oven to 350°F.

Heat a large cast-iron skillet over medium-high heat and add enough oil to generously coat the bottom of the pan.

Carefully place the chops in the skillet. Keep an eye on the meat; often it will contract when it hits the heat and create a concave surface over the pan. Using a spoon or spatula, hold the center of the meat down so that it sears evenly. Once the meat is golden brown, turn over and repeat.

Once browned on the second side, transfer the meat to a cooling rack placed over a baking sheet and roast in the oven. Use a cake tester to test for doneness after about 15 minutes (see page 252); the cake tester should feel just hot enough that you can keep it on your lip for about 1 second, about 135°F for medium-rare.

When your meat is done, allow it to rest in a warm place for almost half of its total cooking time.

Reheat the skillet over medium heat and add the butter. When the butter foams, add the pork back to the pan, and carefully tip the pan toward you and baste the chops with a spoon. Allow the pork to rest another minute or two before slicing. Sprinkle with a pinch of sea salt and serve with the applesauce.

CHARRED APPLESAUCE

MAKES 1 PINT

This is a great larder staple. The smokiness from charring takes away some of the apples' natural tartness, making this just as delicious on top of a pork chop or duck breast for dinner as it is on yogurt for breakfast. All the caramelized sugars give this a rich, complex taste, and the charred bits add smokiness. Just make sure you're using good apples, and you won't need more than a little cider and cinnamon. No other prep or special equipment required.

---

4 apples, such as Braeburn, Cortland, or Fuji (or ask your farmer for recommendations)

Splash of good-quality apple cider, more if needed

1 cinnamon stick

Salt

Honey (optional)

Preheat your oven to 400°F and line a rimmed baking sheet with foil.

Line your stovetop with foil to avoid a big cleanup later. Arrange the apples, unpeeled, on your stove's burners. (If you have an electric stove, you can broil the apples instead—just place the rack close to the broiler and keep an eye on the apples.) They might be hard to balance on the grates at first, but don't be tempted to use a cooling rack as a stabilizer, especially if yours is made of thinner metal. It might melt. Hit the apples with high heat, occasionally turning the apples, and allow all four sides of the apple to blacken, about 1 minute per side.

Once the apples are pretty evenly charred, transfer them to the baking sheet and throw them in the oven. Roast until a cake tester easily slides into the flesh, usually 30 to 40 minutes, but check every 10 minutes or so to gauge their progress; some apples cook much faster than others. Remove from the oven and allow them to cool enough to handle.

Using your hands, separate the skins from the flesh and set aside. They should fall away pretty easily. Using a spoon and/or your fingers, scoop the flesh into a bowl, discarding core and seeds. At this point it's basically already a nice and chunky applesauce, but you can adjust the consistency to your liking. Adding a splash of cider will loosen it up a bit, but bear in mind that it will thicken as it sits in the fridge.

Of the skin you've put aside, sort out about a quarter of it, choosing some of the more charred pieces. Give it a rough chop, then add it into the bowl. Grate in some cinnamon and add salt, both to taste. If you want it sweeter, add honey.

BRAISED FENNEL WITH MINT

SERVES 4

When braising vegetables—or anything for that matter—you soften them slowly and gently in liquid, which deepens their flavor. Normally fennel's crunchy texture and bright, licorice-like flavor make it seem more like a warm-weather vegetable, but bathed in a warm oven for 30 to 40 minutes, it becomes sweet and woodsy. Add some mint and it's a subtly refreshing accompaniment to the deliciously fatty pork.

---

2 large fennel bulbs

Grapeseed or vegetable oil

3 sprigs fresh thyme

1 tablespoon coriander seeds

¼ cup Chardonnay or other rich white wine

½ cup vegetable stock

Salt

Handful of fresh mint leaves, chopped

Preheat the oven to 350°F.

Trim the fennel where the bulb meets the fronds. Chop and reserve some of the fronds to use later as a garnish. Slice the fennel bulb across its "waistline" to get relatively thick rings, about ½ inch thick.

Get a large cast-iron skillet hot over a high flame, add enough oil to coat the bottom, then add the fennel. Cook until it just starts to brown, about 3 minutes.

Meanwhile, warm the thyme and coriander seeds in the bottom of a roasting pan over medium heat. Pull them off the flame once you smell them, about 1 minute.

Add the wine and stock to the herbs. Raise the heat to high and bring the mixture to a boil. Salt the liquid to taste. Add the fennel rings in an even layer at the bottom of the pan. Reduce to a simmer, cover the pan with foil, and put it in the oven. Cook until the fennel is softened but still has a little crunch (you don't want total mush), 35 to 40 minutes.

Remove the fennel from the pan, toss with the mint, and garnish with some of the reserved fronds.

ROASTED NEW POTATOES

SERVES 6

This is a classic cooking method that makes a simple vegetable taste incredible. All cooks should have a solid roast potato recipe in their rotation.

2 pounds small (about 1½ inches in diameter) new or baby red potatoes

Extra-virgin olive oil

Salt and freshly ground black pepper

4 garlic cloves

Leaves from 4 sprigs fresh thyme

Coarse salt (optional)

Preheat the oven to 425°F.

Wash the potatoes under cool water and dry them. Toss them in enough oil to coat completely, and place them on a foil-lined baking sheet. Season gently with salt and pepper. Roast for 20 minutes, then add the garlic and thyme and roast for another 50 to 60 minutes, stirring the potatoes every 15 minutes to keep from charring. Test the potatoes for doneness by inserting a cake tester; they are done when you don't encounter any resistance. Remove the garlic cloves if you don't wish to eat them, but eating them is great as long as you don't plan on kissing anyone. Taste a potato, and if desired, finish with a bit of coarse salt.

LILLIE'S STICKY TOFFEE PUDDING

SERVES 12 TO 16

Lillie started making this dessert growing up in Melbourne, Australia. As she tells it: "It was one of the first puddings my mum showed me how to make and we usually had it on Sunday nights after a roast dinner. I loved it: It was so homely, but tasty. I forgot about sticky toffee pudding until I moved to London and started making it at St. John Bread and Wine. I realized it was actually an English dessert rather than Australian, among many other dishes we like to claim. Now that I'm so far from my family, I love to make this to remind me of home."

FOR THE CAKE

½ pound dates, pitted and chopped

1½ teaspoons baking soda

9 tablespoons unsalted butter, softened, plus more for greasing the pan

1 cup sugar

3 large eggs

2 cups minus 2 tablespoons self-rising flour, plus more for preparing the pan

FOR THE SAUCE

13 tablespoons unsalted butter

2½ cups packed brown sugar

5 cups heavy cream

FOR SERVING

1 cup chopped, toasted pecans (optional)

Preheat the oven to 350°F.

Make the cake: In a medium saucepan, bring 1¼ cups of water plus the dates to a boil. Add the baking soda and remove from the heat. (Don't stir.) Allow to cool completely.

Grease and flour a 12- to 14-inch cast-iron skillet and set aside.

In a large bowl or in the bowl of a stand mixer with the paddle attachment, cream together the butter and sugar. Add in the eggs one at a time, beating until light and fluffy. Add the date mixture and fold in the flour.

Pour the batter into the skillet and cover with foil. Bake for 20 to 30 minutes, or until a cake tester comes out almost clean. A few small pieces of the cake sticking to the tester means it will be moist. Remove from the oven and set on a cooling rack.

Make the sauce: While the cake is baking, melt the butter in a large saucepan over medium heat. Add the brown sugar, stirring until it has been absorbed. Pour in the cream, bring to a boil, and cook until the mixture turns a butterscotch color. Remove from the heat.

Use a fork to poke small holes all over the cake. Pour some warm sauce over the top, allowing it to absorb for 20 minutes. Top with toasted pecans and, if desired, more sauce.

SPRING

DINNER 11

Lavender-Infused Olive Oil–Poached Cod

Braised Fingerling Potatoes

Pea Puree

Charred Spring Onions

WHAT TO DRINK

A dry white wine, such as Crémant du Jura,
Sancerre, or Pouilly-Fumé

LAVENDER-INFUSED OLIVE OIL–POACHED COD

SERVES 4

The best part about this dish is that it takes the effort of preparing fish out of the equation. Searing fish is such a finesse game—there are so many factors you need to nail. If the oil's too hot, you'll overcook the fish. Too cool and it sticks to the pan. But with oil poaching, the fish doesn't dry out because it's being cooked really gently, and it takes on great flavor from the aromatics that infuse into the oil. We particularly like using cod here because of its silky texture.

---

4 (2-by-4-inch) cod fillets

Salt and freshly ground black pepper

About 4 cups extra-virgin olive oil, as needed to submerge fish

1 sprig fresh rosemary

3 sprigs fresh lavender, or 1 tablespoon dried lavender, plus a few sprigs for garnish

½ garlic clove

Coarse sea salt

High-quality extra-virgin olive oil, ideally one with grassy notes

Toasted buckwheat or nuts

Preheat the oven to 350°F.

Season the fish with salt and pepper. Pour a little oil in a roasting pan and place the fillets in one layer in the pan. Add enough oil to fully submerge the fish. Throw in the rosemary, lavender, and garlic and place the pan in the oven. Cook for about 15 minutes, checking for doneness about every 5 minutes. A bit of white might ooze out of the fish; this is just protein and it's totally normal. When the fish is done, ready to flake apart but still somewhat translucent in the center, take it out of the pan using a fish spatula and let it rest for 3 minutes.

Pat the fish with a paper towel to remove any excess cooking oil, then finish with sea salt, the high-quality oil, and a scattering of toasted buckwheat (if using).

BRANDADE

SERVES 4

Brandade is a salty, creamy potato-cod puree that makes for a great dip or mashed potato alternative meant for those who seriously like butter. No joke. You can spread it on a piece of toast with some chives or scallions, or throw some leftover Marinated Zucchini and Mint Salad (page 159) on top for a little acidity.

This dish is traditionally made with salt cod that's been soaking for days. So instead of going the normal—and much more time-consuming—route, we use oil-poached cod. It's a smart way to use leftovers from the Lavender-Infused Olive Oil–Poached Cod (page 142).

---

1 head of garlic

Salt and freshly ground black pepper

2 cups milk

¼ to ½ pound (1 to 2 sticks) unsalted butter

1½ pounds fingerling potatoes, or other small waxy potato

2 tablespoons Dijon mustard

1 to 2 cod fillets, cooked using the method from Olive Oil–Poached Cod (page 142)

Preheat the oven to 300°F.

Slice the top off the head of garlic. Sprinkle the exposed cloves with salt and pepper, then wrap in foil. Roast for 45 minutes to 1 hour, or until the cloves are completely soft. Let cool and reserve half the cloves to use another time (spread on toast, in a sandwich—you get the idea). Smash the garlic cloves into a paste using the side of your knife. Set aside.

In a small saucepan, slowly melt the milk and butter together over low heat. We generally like to use the ratio of 2 parts milk to 1 part butter. Remove from the heat and reserve.

In a large saucepan, place the potatoes in just enough cold water to cover and bring to a boil. Reduce to a simmer and cook until a fork or cake tester slides in easily.

Drain the saucepan and mash the potatoes until smooth and creamy. A food mill works best, but if you don't have one, use a masher or ricer.

Transfer the mashed potatoes back to the saucepan. Over low heat, whisk the potatoes as you add in the milk-butter mixture, one ladle at a time, until you get a creamy texture that can hold a soft peak. Fold in the mustard.

Remove from the heat and add salt and roasted garlic to taste. Flake in your poached fish and gently fold the mixture to incorporate, adjusting seasoning with salt to taste.

BRAISED FINGERLING POTATOES

SERVES 4 TO 6

Small potatoes like fingerlings are fantastic when braised in stock or broth. Especially broth flavored with mushrooms and bacon.

---

2 pounds fingerling potatoes

Salt

2 sprigs fresh thyme

2 sprigs fresh rosemary

3 garlic cloves

2 cups Bacon-Mushroom Broth (page 69) or chicken stock, plus more as needed

Salt

2 tablespoons unsalted butter, cut into chunks (optional)

Coarse sea salt and freshly ground black pepper

If your potatoes are bigger than 2 inches thick, halve them lengthwise.

Place the potatoes in a pan that's deep and wide enough to accommodate all of them in one layer (a roasting pan is perfect). Season with salt. Add the thyme, rosemary, and garlic to the pan, then pour in just enough stock to cover.

Over medium-high heat, bring the stock to a simmer and cook for about 25 minutes or until the potatoes are easily pierced with a fork or cake tester. Remove the potatoes and aromatics from the pot.

Reduce the cooking liquid at a simmer for 5 to 8 minutes, or until it is the consistency of a gravy. Stir in the butter (if using) to make the reduction even richer. Pour the sauce over the potatoes, finish with sea salt and pepper, and serve immediately.

PEA PUREE

SERVES 4

The beauty of simple vegetable purees doesn't stop with hearty vegetables; something as delicate as a fresh pea can shine with a quick cook and a little time in a blender.

4 cups shelled fresh peas

2 cups chicken or vegetable stock, or Bacon-Mushroom Broth (page 69)

Salt

Start by blanching the peas. Fill a large bowl with ice and water. Bring a large pot of generously salted water to a boil over high heat and toss in the peas. Let them cook for about 1 minute, or until tender. To check, scoop out a few and taste them. They should be creamy in the middle yet still have a little "bite." Strain the peas and put them directly into the ice bath to cool completely.

Heat the stock in a small saucepan until warm but not hot. Transfer the peas to a blender or food processor. Add the stock and blend until smooth. Season with salt to taste. Let the puree come to room temperature before serving.

CHARRED SPRING ONIONS

SERVES 4

In Catalonia, Chris was lucky to witness something Catalans go crazy over called *calçots*, which is basically their version of a charred spring onion. (There is even a name for gathering especially to eat this: a *calçotada*.) The cooking method is simple: Make a hot fire, put the spring onions on a grill right on top of the hot flames, and then blacken. Once finished, you peel the outside burned layers away, and you are left with a soft smoky onion that you will never forget. Although our version is a bit different, it's our homage to Catalonia.

These are great done on the grill, but you can also make them in a cast-iron skillet on the stove. You can tell spring onions from green onions or scallions by their larger white bulb, which has a sweeter flavor.

Grapeseed or vegetable oil

8 small spring onions, quartered

Olive oil

Salt

Heat your grill until smoking hot, then use your grill brush to scour off any bits from the grate. Roll up a dish towel, coat it lightly with grapeseed oil (key word being *lightly*; you don't want to start a grease fire), and rub it along the grate so your food doesn't stick.

Toss the spring onions in olive oil and season with salt.

Cover half the surface of your grill with aluminum foil. This is so the more delicate green half of the onion won't overcook, since it cooks much more quickly. Place the onion horizontally so that the green part rests on the foil but the bulb is directly on the grate. Grill until there's a good sear on the onion and it is crisp-tender on the inside.

If you don't have a grill, no worries—just char the onion in a cast-iron skillet, green part and all.

PICKLING

Pickling fruits and vegetables is one of the oldest food-preserving techniques that's stood the test of time. We found manuals issued by the United States Department of Agriculture dating back to 1910 explaining how to pickle produce, and the method goes back centuries longer than that. Some things don't change 'cause they're just that good!

Following is our go-to recipe for pickling. It's super-easy—you just make a simple brine and submerge vegetables or fruit in it—and a great way to get even more mileage out of produce when it's at its peak season. We also use pickles a lot in our food because they add bright acidity to a dish without calling for vinegar, lemon, or more salt.

The measurements that follow are just your basic ratio for making a brine. You can make any adjustments that you like or better suit what you're making. You can throw in any aromatics, such as whole cumin seeds, fennel seeds, coriander seeds, garlic, rosemary, and so on. You can also play with the type of vinegar you use. For example, in our Oysters with Charred Scallions and Pickled Mustard Seeds (page 196), the seeds replace a traditional mignonette, which uses sherry wine vinegar. So we use that vinegar in the recipe for the mustard seeds. Since some vinegars are sweeter than others, start small with the sugar and adjust as needed.

From there, you can decide whether you want to brine something hot or cold. Hot pickling liquid is better at breaking down heartier vegetables like carrots, but it can be too intense for something more delicate—like tomatoes—and cause them to turn to mush. In that case, just let your liquid cool completely before adding it to the produce.

The amounts that follow use a quart container as a measure instead of cups, so all you have to do is eyeball the quantities.

SWEET AND SOUR PICKLE BRINE

MAKES 1 QUART OF PICKLING LIQUID

¼ quart sugar

⅓ quart vinegar (rice wine, Chardonnay, red wine? Your call)

1 teaspoon salt

1 tablespoon freshly ground black pepper

1 to 1½ tablespoons (about as much as will sit on a flattened palm) of aromatics, such as whole cumin seeds, fennel seeds, coriander seeds, garlic, or rosemary (optional)

Suggested vegetables: Cucumbers (such as Kirbys), radishes, trimmed green beans, thin slices of red onion

Add the sugar, vinegar, and ⅔ quart water to a medium saucepan and bring to a simmer. Cook until the sugar has fully dissolved. Remove from the heat.

Taste your pickling liquid. The vinegar should be strong enough to make the back of your throat tickle but not enough so that you cough. Add the salt and pepper and taste for seasoning—you want just enough to round out the acidity of the pickling liquid and bring out its sweetness. Then add the aromatics (if desired).

Situate your produce in either four small (1-cup) or one large (4-cup) mason jar or another glass container with a tightly fitting lid. Make sure there is about 1 inch clearance between the produce and the top of the container.

Either pour the hot brine over your produce now or wait until it's cooled, entirely submerging the produce and keeping ½ inch of clearance. Store in the fridge for up to 3 weeks. If your produce starts to have an almost carbonated taste, that means it's beginning to ferment and should be thrown away. If your vegetables have turned black or brown, the pickles are ready to be tossed.

DINNER 12

Raw Bay Scallops with Seared Pea Shoots
and Grapefruit-Soy Vinaigrette

———

Crisp Soft-Shell Crabs with Fried Capers
and Parsley Vinaigrette

———

Marinated Zucchini and Mint Salad

———

Bowl of Cherries

WHAT TO DRINK

Super-dry Brut Zero or Extra Brut Champagne
or a light Sonoma Chardonnay

RAW BAY SCALLOPS
WITH SEARED PEA SHOOTS
AND GRAPEFRUIT-SOY VINAIGRETTE
SERVES 4 TO 6

Good bay scallops are incredible. They're small, sweet, and briny, almost creamy. If you see them at a good fish market, make a move for them, but ask first if they have been "dipped." Dipped scallops have been treated with a preservative that plumps them up with water, which means you're paying for dead weight and a metallic taste. But a good bay scallop's natural brine is really nice, so why mess with it? The sautéed pea shoots—or early stems of a pea plant, also called pea tendrils—plus the vinaigrette then bring smoke, citrus, and salt to the dish.

Grapeseed or vegetable oil

1 handful of pea shoots

Salt

1 tablespoon soy sauce

1 tablespoon freshly squeezed grapefruit juice

Splash of stock or water

Extra-virgin olive oil

Freshly ground black pepper

20 bay scallops (about ¼ to ½ pound)

Fleur de sel or other light finishing salt

Shiso, sliced thin, for garnish

Togarashi pepper (Japanese 7 spice)

Set a large sauté pan over high heat. When it's smoking hot, add just enough grapeseed oil to coat the bottom and quickly sear your pea shoots. While the pea shoots are in the pan, season them carefully with salt—they don't require a lot. When they've gotten a bit of color, remove them from the pan and place them on a paper towel to drain. Transfer them to a bowl and place them in the fridge to cool for a few minutes.

While the pea shoots are cooling, make your vinaigrette. Add the soy sauce, grapefruit juice, the stock, and about 3 tablespoons of olive oil to a mason jar. Cover, give it a good shake, and season with salt and pepper to taste.

On each plate, lay down the pea shoots, then the scallops. Make sure to dress each individual scallop with a bit of fleur de sel and then drizzle the vinaigrette over the top. To finish, top each plate with a pinch of shiso and Togarashi pepper.

CRISP SOFT-SHELL CRABS
WITH FRIED CAPERS AND PARSLEY VINAIGRETTE

SERVES 4 TO 6

Soft-shell crabs always taste better if you buy them while they're still alive. Take the time to either clean them yourself (ask your fishmonger how to do this when you buy them) or have him do it for you so they are alive until just before you cook them. Store them in the refrigerator covered with a damp towel (not on ice or they'll get waterlogged).

---

1 whole head of garlic, plus 2 to
3 additional cloves, smashed

Salt and freshly ground black pepper

½ small white onion, roughly chopped

½ bunch of fresh parsley, roughly chopped

½ cup champagne vinegar

½ cup fresh lemon juice

2½ cups extra-virgin olive oil

Grapeseed or vegetable oil

½ cup capers, rinsed and blotted very dry

8 soft-shell crabs

Wondra flour

4 tablespoons (½ stick) unsalted butter

4 cups arugula, washed and dried
(see page 255)

¼ cup thinly sliced chives (optional)

2 lemons, cut into wedges

Preheat the oven to 300°F.

Slice the top off the head of garlic. Sprinkle the exposed cloves with salt and pepper, then wrap in foil. Roast for 45 minutes to 1 hour, or until the cloves are completely soft.

Place 2 cloves of the roasted garlic (save the rest for another use), the onion, parsley, vinegar, and lemon juice in a blender and blend until smooth. With the motor running, slowly pour in the olive oil until the mixture is emulsified but still loose. Taste and adjust the flavor by adding more oil or vinegar, if necessary, and season with salt and pepper. Set aside.

In a small saucepan, heat enough grapeseed oil to generously coat the bottom over medium heat. When the oil shimmers, add the capers and fry until just brown. Transfer them to a paper-towel-lined plate or bowl to drain.

Coat the bottom of a large cast-iron or heavy-bottomed skillet with oil and heat over a medium flame. You'll know the oil is hot enough when it starts to "dance" or shimmer. Dust the crabs with Wondra, then place them top side down in the skillet, making sure not to crowd them or they won't get crispy. If you have to, work in batches. Season the belly with salt and pepper—but use a light hand, since crabs are naturally salty. Cook the crabs in the skillet until they're golden brown. After 4 to 5 minutes, you can use a thin spatula or spoon to check on the progress. Flip them over and repeat for a total cook time of about 8 minutes. To finish, add the butter, along with the smashed garlic cloves. Baste the crabs with the foaming butter until the butter is brown. Remove the crabs from the skillet and set aside.

Toss the arugula with a few spoonfuls of the vinaigrette to taste, and plate with the crabs. Top with a good pinch of capers per plate and chives, too (if using). Serve with a bowl of lemon wedges to squeeze over the crab.

MARINATED ZUCCHINI
AND MINT SALAD
SERVES 4

This is one of those great no-brainer warm-weather salads. All you need is 1 zucchini per person. Get a bunch of different varieties and mix up each plate.

---

4 zucchini or summer squash

2 to 3 tablespoons extra-virgin olive oil

¼ cup champagne vinegar

⅓ cup fresh oregano leaves, plus extra for garnish

⅓ cup chopped fresh mint, plus extra for garnish

1 medium shallot, thinly sliced

Salt and freshly ground black pepper

⅔ cup crushed almonds or pistachios (optional)

Slice the zucchini as thinly as possible (a mandoline is handy here), and toss the strips with just enough oil to coat, the champagne vinegar, and herbs, and allow the whole thing to sit in the fridge for a couple of hours. The vinegar will "cook" the squash a little bit, softening it a touch but still preserving its fresh crispness. Strain out the juices that have accumulated, add the shallot and season with salt and pepper to taste, and sprinkle the almonds on top (if using).

BOWL OF
CHERRIES
SERVES 1 TO A CROWD

Sometimes the best dessert is as simple as a bowl of perfectly ripened fruit, grown locally and picked at the peak of its season. For a little something extra, serve these with crème fraîche on the side.

Cherries, as desired

Put the cherries in a bowl. Serve.

DINNER 13

Grilled Radicchio and Peaches

Crisp Brick Chicken

Ithai's Kind-of Sundae

WHAT TO DRINK

Peach Porch Punch

A light red, such as Pinot Noir

PEACH PORCH PUNCH

MAKES 5 COCKTAILS, BUT FEEL FREE TO DOUBLE THE RECIPE

As fun as it is to shake and stir a cocktail for yourself and your friends, no one wants to be handcuffed to the bar or kitchen when everyone else is out having fun. Whether you're lying out on the porch, sitting at the foot of the river, or working in the garden, it's nice to have a big pitcher of punch that everyone can serve themselves from. This recipe has aspects of all the classic porch drinks like iced teas and lemonades, as well as the summer classics of juleps and greyhounds. Help yourself! —*Nino*

---

4 bags of strong white peach tea

1 cup loosely packed fresh mint leaves, plus more for garnish

¼ cup sugar, preferably demerara for its richness

½ cup fresh grapefruit juice

½ cup fresh lemon juice

2 cups aged rum

6 dashes Angostura bitters

Club soda

Citrus and peach rounds

Fill a medium freezer-safe bowl or a plastic pint container with water and place in the freezer until frozen solid.

Bring 3 cups of water to a boil and add the tea bags, mint, and sugar. Turn off the heat and steep for 15 minutes. Strain into a large bowl and let cool. Add the grapefruit juice, lemon juice, rum, and bitters. Stir well and refrigerate.

About 15 minutes before serving, add the large ice cube to the punch as well as a few splashes of club soda. Garnish with the fruit rounds and some mint.

GRILLED RADICCHIO AND PEACHES

SERVES 4

Before writing a cookbook ever became a reality, this was one of the first dishes we would cook for our friends. The inspiration for the dish came about mostly because peaches were perfectly in season, and frankly, it just sounded fun to pair sweet peaches with the nutty and smoky grilled radicchio. So that's just what we did, and here it is.

Grapeseed or vegetable oil

1 teaspoon Dijon mustard

¼ garlic clove, grated or minced

Salt and freshly ground black pepper

2 anchovy fillets, minced (optional)

½ cup red wine vinegar

1¼ cups extra-virgin olive oil, plus more as needed

2 heads of radicchio, halved (Treviso, the thinner variety, is great)

2 large peaches, halved and pitted

Heat your grill until smoking hot, then use your grill brush to scour off any bits from the grate. Roll up a dish towel and coat it lightly with grapeseed oil, and rub it along the grate so your food doesn't stick.

In a mason jar, combine the mustard, garlic, a good pinch of salt, and a couple of grinds of pepper. If you want to take the vinaigrette up a notch, add the minced anchovy, too. (It's really good with grilled radicchio.) Add the vinegar and olive oil, then shake to emulsify. Taste, and adjust with salt, pepper, vinegar, or olive oil.

Toss the radicchio and peaches with a good splash of olive oil, season with salt and pepper, and lay them on a hot grill until just charred. Flip and repeat. Remove from the grill and set aside.

Slice the radicchio and peaches into smaller, bite-size pieces and toss with a few spoonfuls of the vinaigrette. Leftover vinaigrette keeps in the refrigerator for up to 10 days.

CRISP BRICK CHICKEN

SERVES 4

You've probably heard of this method for searing chicken for the obvious reason—the brick. And maybe in the past that's sounded a little scary or complicated. But the truth is, you don't need a brick. All that matters is having some kind of weight on the chicken because that's what's going to give you a perfect sear and also cook the bird evenly. Go with your weight of choice—multiple pans, a rock, a dumbbell on top of a pan—it really doesn't make a difference as long as it's about 7 pounds, or enough to press the chicken completely and evenly. You can ask your butcher to "spatchcock" (or halve, butterfly, and debone) your chicken, so it lays flat. Ideally he or she would leave in the leg bones, since they offer a lot of flavor, but no worries if that doesn't happen.

---

1 chicken (2 to 3 pounds), halved and deboned, preferably with leg bones left in

Grapeseed or vegetable oil

Salt and freshly ground black pepper

2 generous tablespoons unsalted butter

4 garlic cloves

½ sprig fresh rosemary

2 fresh sage leaves (optional)

½ lemon

Coarse sea salt

Preheat the oven to 350°F.

Take the chicken out of the fridge about 45 minutes before cooking to allow the meat to come to room temperature. Have your weight handy, making sure it is clean and not ice cold. Dry the chicken very well with paper towels. Set up a roasting pan or rimmed baking sheet with a roasting rack.

Set a very large, heavy skillet (big enough to take the whole flattened chicken) over medium-high heat, and add enough oil to coat the bottom. (If you don't have a pan large enough, split the chicken in half, down the spine, and use two heavy pans.) Season the chicken thoroughly with salt and pepper. When your oil starts to smoke, place the chicken in the pan, skin side down. "Spin" (don't flip) the chicken so that the oil underneath it evens out (see Carrying the Sear on page 253), then place your weight on top of the chicken. After about 4 minutes, check your sear. You're looking for an even and beautiful golden brown. Once there, flip the chicken over and repeat for another 4 minutes or until golden.

Remove the weight and transfer the chicken to the roasting rack skin side up. Put the chicken in the oven and cook until a cake tester feels hot, or a thermometer indicates an internal temperature of 150°F to 155°F, 15 to 20 minutes.

Remove the chicken from the oven and allow it to rest for 5 to 10 minutes, flipping halfway through.

Rinse and wipe out the pan you used to sear the chicken, and heat over medium-high heat. When hot, add the butter and throw in the garlic and herbs. When the butter starts foaming, add the chicken, tip the pan gently toward you, and *arroser* the chicken with the foaming butter for a good 30 seconds to a minute (see *arroser*, page 251). Put the chicken back on the cooling rack, and finish with a squeeze of lemon, a sprinkle of sea salt, and some grindings of pepper. Allow it to rest 1 more minute, then serve.

ITHAI'S KIND-OF SUNDAE

SERVES 1 TO A CROWD

I'm not normally that into sweets, but this is the kind of dessert I'll itch for while watching the Knicks game or in need of a late snack. Growing up, if we didn't have coffee ice cream in the freezer—which was my family's go-to flavor—I'd grab vanilla ice cream instead and mix in some Folgers instant coffee. As I started cooking more and more and noticing how often pastry chefs were throwing salt on their dishes, I added salt to the mix. It balances out the flavor and creates complexity at the same time. I guess we can call it a sundae, but really it's just a modified scoop of ice cream.

This recipe calls for vanilla ice cream, but you can definitely make this with coffee ice cream, hazelnut, pistachio, fruit-flavored—whatever's your jam. Also, the better coffee you use, the better this'll be. When I go out to eat, I'll ask for a demitasse of ground espresso. (Yeah, this dish is so good you'll even want to make it when you go out to eat.) But this is also a great excuse to use the Folgers that's been sitting in your pantry forever. And as for salt, ideally you'd use something with big flakes like Maldon salt.

Scoop some vanilla ice cream into a bowl. Top with a dusting of instant coffee and a small pinch of salt. If you have corn flakes lying around, throw those in, too. The crunch can't hurt, right? Dig in.

DINNER 14

Roasted Lamb Chops

———

Sautéed Ramps

———

Spiced Carrots and Harissa Yogurt

———

Mina's Olive Oil–Walnut Cake

WHAT TO DRINK

Spicy Loire red with high acid,
such as Pineau d'Aunis or Gamay

ROASTED LAMB CHOPS

SERVES 2 TO 4

We really prefer buying whole racks of lamb rather than individual chops. That way, you can just cook one rack instead of many chops, and you can get a better sear without overcooking the meat. Try to avoid buying a rack that's been "frenched," or has had the meat stripped away from the rib bones. Sure, it looks pretty and makes for a nice little handle to eat with, but why would you want to throw away all that delicious fat when it could be seeping into the meat while it's cooking? Lamb fat is tasty, so don't let it go to waste just for aesthetic purposes.

Ask your butcher to make sure that the spine is fully removed, including the "eye" bones. Sometimes these bones are missed, and they could end up chipping your knife when you cut up the chops. And be sure to buy the rack the day before so that you can marinate it for a good 24 hours.

---

1 rack of lamb (about 8 chops)

4 garlic cloves, smashed

4 sprigs fresh rosemary

Grapeseed or vegetable oil

Salt

2 generous tablespoons unsalted butter

Coarse sea salt

Place the lamb, garlic, and rosemary into a large plastic zipper-lock bag. Add enough oil to coat everything evenly and then do your best to squeeze out as much of the air as possible out of the bag. You're trying to mimic a vacuum seal so the garlic and rosemary flavors have nowhere to go but into the lamb. Refrigerate for 24 hours.

About an hour before you're ready to cook the lamb, pull the bag out of the fridge, remove the lamb, and pat it dry with paper towels. Pick off any garlic and rosemary sticking to the lamb and reserve; discard the marinade. Let the lamb come to room temperature.

Preheat the oven to 350°F.

When you're ready to start cooking, grab a large cast-iron pan, pour in enough oil to coat the bottom, and get it very hot over high heat. Season the lamb heavily with salt. We usually do this in the sink so that we can make it rain salt without making a mess.

When the oil is just about smoking, tip your pan away from you so that the hot oil doesn't splatter you and place the rack, fat side down, in the pan. Let the lamb sear until golden brown, about 2 minutes, then flip and sear the other side. Transfer the lamb to a roasting rack or rack placed inside a rimmed baking pan and roast in the oven. After about 10 minutes, check your meat with a cake tester (see page 252). Depending on the size of your rack, cooking times will differ, so checking is the best way to know where you're at. You'll want the tester to feel just-warm to warm.

Remove the lamb from the oven and allow it to rest on a cooling rack in a warm place for half of your total cooking time.

Over medium heat, melt the butter in the first pan you used, throwing in the rosemary and garlic from the marinade. Add the lamb, tip the pan gently toward you, and baste with foaming butter for a good 30 seconds. Rest the rack again for another minute.

When you're ready to cut up the chops, put the fat side of the rack down flat on your cutting board so that the bones are easily visible. Use them as a guide for your knife, cutting along the bones to separate each chop.

Finish the chops with a dash of sea salt and serve immediately.

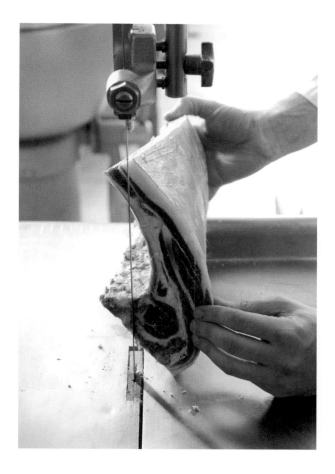

RAMPS

Ramps, or wild leeks, are found mostly in the eastern United States and are one of the best things that grow naturally in New York. So it is no surprise that everyone goes nuts for the one month they are in season. You'd be hard-pressed to find a menu without them—sautéed, grilled, pickled, you name it. Yes, the hype can get annoying, but it's for good reason. Their pungent, almost garlicky flavor makes them just as versatile as they are delicious. It's actually sad how quickly they come and go.

To help take full advantage of when ramps are out in full force—and also preserve their unique flavor well beyond—we enlisted our friend Ash Merriman. She's one of Ithai's closest friends and also happens to be one of the best chefs we know. She heads up kitchens in New York City and if you haven't heard of her already, we're sure you will soon.

SAUTÉED RAMPS

SERVES 4

For a short time in the spring, when ramps are in season, what's in the fridge often doesn't look as appealing as grabbing some ramps out of the woods. (If you do forage for them, though, take care not to take more than 15 to 20 percent from one spot; ideally, you'll take the leaves only—a single leaf from each plant, and leave the bulbs to grow.) Their flavor is the perfect mix of garlic and onion with just a little sweetness, so you don't need to do much to them to make something delicious—just clean and sauté them. See Ramps (above) for a variety of ways to use them.

Grapeseed or vegetable oil

4 generous handfuls of ramps (white and green parts)

Pinch of salt

Coat a large cast-iron skillet with oil, and heat over high heat until it shimmers. Throw in the ramps and add salt. Sauté until just wilted. Remove from the heat and serve.

RAMP COMPOUND BUTTER

MAKES 1 POUND

I like to make this butter at the beginning of ramp season when the bulbs are tiny and the pungent ramp kick has yet to gain full throttle. It is the one time I use raw ramps, and their soft onion flavor permeates the butter. If it's later in the season, I recommend cooking your ramps quickly before making the butter. Slather it on steak, chicken, toast with avocado, crackers—you name it.

---

12 to 15 small ramps (white and green parts), cleaned

1 pound (4 sticks) unsalted butter, softened

1 small shallot, finely minced

Grated zest of 1 small lemon

Salt and freshly ground black pepper

Trim the small white roots from the ends of the ramps and separate the bulbs from the green leaves. Finely mince the bulbs and chiffonade (see page 255) the tops.

Place all ingredients in the bowl of a stand mixer fitted with the paddle attachment. Mix until all the ingredients are incorporated well.

Divide the butter mixture in half onto two sheets of parchment paper or plastic wrap. Form logs by tightly wrapping the parchment or plastic wrap around the butter. Store in an airtight container or freezer bags. The butter will keep in the fridge for a few days or up to a month in the freezer.

QUICK RAMP RELISH

MAKES ABOUT 4 CUPS

Make a batch of this using our simple pickling method (see page 151), then throw this spread on sandwiches, toast, burgers—anywhere that would benefit from a little briny, oniony, garlicky kick. The pickles will take time to reach their peak flavor, so try to give them about a week before you dig in.

½ cup sugar

⅔ cup rice wine, white wine, or red wine vinegar

Salt and freshly ground black pepper

1 teaspoon brown mustard seeds

1 teaspoon yellow mustard seeds

¼ teaspoon coriander seeds, toasted

¼ sprig fresh dill, chopped

1½ cups finely chopped ramps (white and green parts)

¼ red onion, finely chopped

1 medium green tomato, charred on the grill, in the oven, or in a cast-iron skillet; peeled and roughly chopped

1 Kirby cucumber, peeled, seeded, and roughly chopped

Add the sugar, 1¼ cups water, and vinegar to a medium pot and bring to a simmer. Cook until the sugar has fully dissolved. Remove from the heat.

(recipe continues)

175

Taste your pickling liquid. The vinegar should be strong enough to make the back of your throat tickle, but not enough so that you cough. Season to taste with salt and pepper, then add the brown mustard seeds, yellow mustard seeds, coriander seeds, and dill.

Divide the ramps, onion, green tomato, and cucumber into glass containers with tight-fitting lids, leaving an inch of space at the top. Wait until the liquid has cooled, then pour it over the vegetables, submerging them completely, leaving ½ inch of space. (Keeping the liquid cool gives you crunchy ramps, and it preserves their pink and white colors. If you prefer the ramps wilted, pour the liquid in while hot.) Store in the fridge.

RAMP REMOULADE

MAKES ABOUT 2½ CUPS

Remoulade is basically dressed-up mayonnaise. It goes really well with meats and is perfect any time you want a more herbaceous alternative to mayo.

1 large egg yolk

½ teaspoon Dijon mustard

½ teaspoon mustard powder

½ teaspoon prepared horseradish

½ tablespoon champagne vinegar

Juice of 1 lemon

Juice of ½ lime

½ teaspoon Tabasco sauce

¼ teaspoon cayenne pepper

2 cups canola oil

¼ cup Quick Ramp Relish (page 175)

1 tablespoon chopped fresh parley

½ small red onion, minced

½ cup fresh ramps (green parts only), blanched and chopped

2 tablespoons capers, roughly chopped

½ teaspoon grainy mustard

Salt and freshly ground black pepper

Place the egg yolk, Dijon mustard, mustard powder, horseradish, vinegar, lemon juice, lime juice, Tabasco sauce, and cayenne in the bowl of a food processor or blender. Blend to combine, then, with the motor running, slowly add the oil into the mixture. Continue to add in all the oil until your mayonnaise has formed.

Transfer the sauce to a large mixing bowl. Using the food processor or blender, quickly pulse the ramp relish to chop, but don't puree it entirely. Scrape the relish into the mayonnaise. Add the parsley, onion, ramps, capers, and grainy mustard. Season to taste with salt and black pepper. Keep in an airtight container in the refrigerator for up to 5 days

SPICED CARROTS AND HARISSA YOGURT

SERVES 4 TO 6

We like adding yogurt in places you wouldn't normally expect because it's such an underrated condiment that absorbs flavors really well, especially spices. In this case, it picks up and mellows out the heat in smoky Moroccan harissa and makes a great complement to sweet carrots.

---

1 head of garlic

Extra-virgin olive oil

1 shallot

Juice of ½ lemon

Salt

8 to 12 medium to small carrots

1 cup plain Greek yogurt

2 tablespoons Moroccan harissa, or to taste (or use paprika and chipotle powder)

½ cup sunflower seeds, toasted

½ cup pistachios, toasted (see page 255)

2 tablespoons chopped fresh parsley

2 tablespoons chiffonaded fresh mint (see page 255)

Preheat the oven to 300°F.

Slice the head of garlic in half widthwise and toss in oil just to coat. Wrap it in foil and bake until a cake tester can easily slide through the cloves, 45 minutes to 1 hour.

Allow it to cool, then squeeze out the cloves from their husks. Using the flat side of your knife, mash the cloves into a paste. Set aside.

Slice the shallot into paper-thin rings and toss in a bowl with just enough lemon juice to coat. Season lightly with salt. Allow to sit for 30 minutes.

Preheat the broiler. Peel the carrots and trim the tops and ends. Cook the carrots in the boiling water until they are just shy of fork-tender. You want them to be a bit undercooked at this point. Remove the carrots and lay them on a baking sheet. Toss them with oil and a little salt. Place the baking sheet under the broiler until the carrots are slightly blistered.

Put the yogurt in a small mixing bowl. Stir in the harissa until you get your desired spice level. Do the same with the roasted garlic paste. Then add the lemon juice and salt to taste. At this point we're looking for a loose consistency for the yogurt. If yours is still too thick, add a little olive oil at a time until you get there.

To serve, spoon some of the yogurt on each plate, put the carrots on top, then finish with sunflower seeds, pistachios, the shallot, parsley, and mint.

MINA'S OLIVE OIL–WALNUT CAKE

SERVES 6 TO 8

One of the first times we hung out together and had people over to eat, our friend Mina brought this cake. We found it to be almost like a tastier, healthier pound cake—rich and dense and kind of fruity and grassy from the olive oil and citrus.

¾ cup olive oil, plus extra for the pan

1 cup all-purpose flour, plus extra for the pan

¼ teaspoon baking powder

¼ teaspoon baking soda

1 teaspoon ground cinnamon, plus more for serving

¼ teaspoon ground cloves

½ teaspoon salt

1 large egg plus 1 yolk

¾ cup plus 1 tablespoon granulated sugar

¼ cup plus 2 tablespoons milk

2 tablespoons brandy or cognac

1½ teaspoons grated orange zest

2 tablespoons freshly squeezed orange juice

1 cup chopped walnuts, toasted (see page 255)

Powdered sugar, for serving (optional)

Preheat the oven to 350°F.

Lightly oil an 8-inch cake pan and lightly dust with flour.

In a large mixing bowl, combine the flour, baking powder, baking soda, cinnamon, cloves, and salt. Stir until just mixed, then make a well in the center. Set aside.

In a separate medium bowl, whisk the egg, egg yolk, and oil until combined. Add the ¾ cup of granulated sugar and whisk well. Whisk in the milk, brandy, orange zest, and orange juice.

Pour the wet mixture into the dry ingredients and whisk, working from the center and moving outward, until the batter is smooth. Fold in the walnuts. Pour the mixture into the prepared pan and sprinkle the top with the remaining tablespoon of granulated sugar.

Bake for about 1 hour, until the top gets crusty and dark brown and a knife or cake tester inserted in the center comes out clean. Slice and serve with a dusting of powdered sugar (if desired) and cinnamon.

DINNER 15

Seared Branzino with Pancetta
and Potato Panzanella

———

Chilled Asparagus, Beet,
and Kohlrabi Broth

WHAT TO DRINK

La Passeggiata

———

A Sauvignon Blanc or
Chenin from Montlouis

LA PASSEGGIATA

MAKES 1 COCKTAIL

This cocktail is named after the traditional evening stroll of Italy. At dusk, Italians take to the streets and piazzas to people-watch, relax, flirt, and to see and be seen.

This is a variation on the godfather of all Italian cocktails: the Negroni. Here, though, I replace the traditional bitter red Campari with Salers, a French aperitif made from roots, herbs, and citrus. It is bitter and sweet with notes of anise and citrus. Also, Cocchi Americano replaces the sweet vermouth. It's delicate and complex with notes of orange flower, pear, honey, and citrus, which balances wonderfully with the Salers. The fennel garnish—known for its magical quality to both stimulate and suppress the appetite (only in Italy!)—rounds this out as the perfect drink for a summer evening. —*Nino*

1½ ounces dry gin

¾ ounce Cocchi Americano

¾ ounce Salers

2 dashes of grapefruit bitters

Slice of fennel or fennel fronds

Stir together the gin, Cocchi Americano, Salers, and bitters over ice until well chilled. Strain into a chilled cocktail glass and garnish with fennel.

SEARED BRANZINO
WITH PANCETTA AND POTATO PANZANELLA

SERVES 4

Panzanella is an Italian word for bread crumb or crouton salad. Normally you see it on summer menus because it's a way to showcase late-summer tomatoes. But this version is better suited for late winter or early spring. That's when you get a second wave of flavorful tomatoes that are grown in hothouses. We know this goes against the always-buy-seasonal mandate, but this is an exception that makes sense. Hothouse tomatoes are a little more tart than the sweet tomatoes of summer and add a nice acidity to a dish, particularly this one. Add in some larder staples, like potatoes and pancetta, and silver fish, like branzino or Spanish mackerel—which is great this time of year—and you've made a summer standby perfect for colder months.

---

12 small waxy potatoes like new potatoes or fingerlings

4 thick slices rustic, crusty bread

Extra-virgin olive oil

Salt and freshly ground black pepper

Pinch of fresh thyme and/or fresh oregano (optional)

1 slice pancetta or bacon (about ¼ inch thick)

1 shallot, thinly sliced

10 cherry tomatoes, quartered

2 pounds branzino or Spanish mackerel fillets

1 lemon

1 orange

Coarse sea salt

Pinch of smoked paprika (optional)

2 tablespoons chopped chives

In a medium saucepan, just cover the potatoes with cold water and bring to a boil over high heat. Generously salt the water to season the potatoes as they cook. Once boiling, reduce to a simmer and cook until the potatoes can be pierced easily by a cake tester, about 20 minutes. Drain the potatoes and set aside to cool.

Slice the bread into ½- to 1-inch cubes. Imagine that you're taking a bite of fish along with it—you want everything to fit on the fork. Generously coat the bottom of a cast-iron or heavy-bottomed skillet with oil. Heat over a medium flame and add the bread, tossing to coat. Season with salt, pepper, and thyme and/or oregano (if using). Keep the bread cubes moving in the pan so they are evenly seasoned and toast to a golden brown. Lay the bread cubes on a paper-towel-lined plate to drain.

Slice your pancetta crosswise into ¼-inch-thick lardons. Then slice again lengthwise into ¼-inch-square cubes.

Wipe out the skillet you just used to toast the bread. Heat over a low flame, add the pancetta, and slowly render out the fat until crisp. Scoop the pieces out onto a paper-towel-lined plate, but keep the fat in the pan—you'll want to use it to cook the rest of the ingredients so everything picks up that nice porky flavor.

Increase the heat to medium and throw in the shallot. Sauté until it has softened a touch with just a hair of color. You can add some oil if the pan starts to look dry. Add the tomatoes.

While the shallot and tomatoes are cooking, crush the potatoes with your palm so they make flattened little patties. Add them to the pan along with the tomatoes and shallot and season with a bit of salt. Cook until the tomatoes have just softened and the potatoes have heated through. Remove the mixture from the pan and transfer to a large bowl. Add the pancetta and bread cubes and gently combine.

Wipe out the skillet and set over medium-high heat with enough oil to coat the bottom. When the oil is shimmering hot, carefully add the branzino fillets to the pan, and salt them. Turn down the heat if they are sizzling like crazy; you want them to be lively, but not screaming. (Be sure not to crowd the fillets; cook in batches if necessary.)

When you see a golden crust form on the bottom of the fish, about 3 minutes, carefully flip the fillets with a thin spatula and lightly salt them. Continue cooking until a cake tester slides into the flesh easily, with almost no resistance, another minute or so. Or go ahead and cut into a piece if you're not sure. (If using Spanish mackerel, which is usually a thin fillet, this may be a matter of seconds.) When the fish is just barely translucent, you're ready. Remove the fish to a warm plate and let it rest for a minute.

While the fish rests, finish the panzanella by giving it a small squeeze of lemon and orange juice, to taste. Add a little coarse salt, and a tiny pinch of paprika, which adds a nice smokiness. (If you're using bacon and it is very smoky, you can omit this.)

Heap the salad onto each plate and top with the fish, skin side up so that it stays crisp. Garnish with a few pinches of chives and serve immediately.

CHILLED ASPARAGUS, BEET, AND KOHLRABI BROTH

SERVES 4

As Chris spent a good part of a year in Germany, one thing he couldn't help noticing is that few people seem to appreciate the coming of asparagus season as much as the Germans. In the springtime, *weis spargel*, or white asparagus, is on every menu in Germany. It is pretty much assumed that if it's in season, you're going to order something with *spargel* in it. After visiting during that time, we started to rack our brains as to how we could create a unique preparation that celebrates asparagus and would make the Germans proud. This soup was the result. We use green asparagus because it's much more common, but if you have white, that would be ideal.

---

6 small beets

Olive oil

Salt and freshly ground black pepper

Leaves from 1 sprig fresh thyme

3 shallots

Grapeseed or vegetable oil

1 slice bacon

1 cup dry white wine (something you'd be okay drinking)

2½ cups vegetable stock

½ bay leaf

8 to 12 medium asparagus stalks

1 small handful of crushed pistachios

1 kohlrabi bulb, peeled and sliced paper thin

1 teaspoon grated orange zest

Coarse sea salt

1 tablespoon chives, thinly sliced

Mustard or chili oil

Trout roe, for garnish (optional)

Preheat the oven to 400°F.

In a mixing bowl, toss the beets with enough olive oil to coat, then season well with salt, pepper, and thyme. Wrap the beets in a foil pouch and roast them in the oven until a cake tester can easily pierce them, about 45 minutes. Allow them to cool to room temperature, then trim off the tops and bottoms and slip the peels away from the flesh. Allow the beets to cool completely in the fridge.

Dice 2 of the shallots and slice the remaining shallot paper thin. In a sauté pan over a low flame, add enough grapeseed oil to coat the bottom. Add the diced shallots and bacon and sweat until the shallots are translucent and the bacon is crispy, 10 to 15 minutes.

Pour in the wine to deglaze the pan, bring to a boil over medium heat, then reduce to a simmer and cook until it reduces to about ½ cup, 7 to 10 minutes. Add the stock and bay leaf, bring to a boil, then reduce to a simmer and cook for about 10 to 15 minutes.

Transfer the mixture to a bowl, removing the bacon, and set in the fridge to cool.

Bring a large pot of water to a boil and add enough salt so that you can taste it. Fill a large bowl with ice and water.

Break off the bottoms of the asparagus. They'll naturally snap where the tougher ends meet the tender part of the stalk. Cook the asparagus for 3 to 5 minutes in the boiling water. It should still be bright green and tender with a bit of crunch. Once done, remove all the asparagus with a slotted spoon and put immediately in the ice bath. Transfer the asparagus to a plate and let chill in the fridge.

Once all your ingredients are cold, cut the asparagus and beets into bite-size pieces. Skim off any fat on the top of the broth and discard the bay leaf. Arrange the vegetables in a shallow bowl and fill it halfway with the broth.

Finish the dish by adding the pistachios, then topping the broth with slices of kohlrabi and shallot, about 3 of each per bowl. Add a pinch of orange zest, a bit of sea salt and chives, and a few drops of mustard oil. Just be careful—too much will truly bust up this dish. If desired, trout roe makes a really nice garnish.

SUMMER

DINNER 16

Oysters with Charred Scallions
and Pickled Mustard Seeds

———————

Grilled Red Cabbage Slaw

———————

The Hamburger

———————

Tal's Potato Salad

WHAT TO DRINK

Bloody Mary

———————

A rich, dirty Syrah, preferably from Rhône
or Central Coast, California

BLOODY MARY

MAKES 1 COCKTAIL

This is a great basic recipe. You can build, add, and adjust depending on your own taste. Add garnishes such as radishes, olives, sweet peppers, hot peppers, pickled vegetables, or our favorite—an oyster. Play with different ingredients like changing the acid component from citrus to vinegar. I really like adding some smoked pimentón for smoky depth or pickle brine to give it a salty kick. —*Nino*

2 ounces vodka

4 ounces tomato juice

½ ounce fresh lemon juice

½ ounce Worcestershire sauce

Pinch of freshly ground black pepper

Pinch of celery salt

2 or 3 dashes of hot sauce

Bar spoonful of prepared horseradish

1 stalk celery

Shake all ingredients except the celery with ice and strain into a glass filled with ice. Garnish with the celery.

OYSTERS
WITH CHARRED SCALLIONS AND PICKLED MUSTARD SEEDS
SERVES 6

Starting a meal with oysters is kind of the best way to get a meal going—everyone gets involved with the shucking, so you can just keep throwing them back. Pickled mustard seeds add a unique element. It almost acts like caviar in its texture, but its flavor is, as you might've guessed, pickled and mustardlike. Keep them in the fridge like a condiment and put them on anything from a rib eye to risotto to add a briny punch.

---

1 cup sherry vinegar

⅓ cup sugar

Salt

½ cup whole mustard seeds

Grapeseed or vegetable oil

½ bunch of scallions, white and green parts, sliced

Freshly ground black pepper

2 dozen oysters, scrubbed

Grated zest of 1 lemon

SPECIAL EQUIPMENT

oyster knife

Combine the vinegar, sugar, and 1¼ cups water in a small saucepan over medium heat. Simmer until the sugar is dissolved. Salt to taste and pour the liquid over the mustard seeds in a small bowl or container. Set aside.

Add enough oil to coat the bottom of a large skillet and heat it over high heat until it shim-

mers. Add as many scallions as will fit in one layer in the pan. Let them sear and wilt. Season to taste with salt and pepper and remove from the heat. Repeat with another batch, if necessary. Once the scallions are cool enough to handle, slice thinly.

On your counter, firmly hold the oyster flat side up between two towels. Notice that there is a point in the back of the oyster where the top and bottom shells come together. Aim the tip of the oyster knife into this joint and use a little force to wedge it in. Gently but firmly, twist the knife to pop the joint open. Run the knife at a slight upward angle along the length of the shell to remove the top shell. Once it's off, inspect the oyster; it should smell sweet like the ocean. If it's dry or has an off aroma, discard it.

Gently scoop the bottom of the oyster meat with the knife to clear it from the shell. Remove any grit with your finger. Sprinkle each oyster with a scallion, a small pile of pickled mustard seeds, a tiny pinch of lemon zest, and a few drops of pickling liquid.

GRILLED RED CABBAGE SLAW

SERVES 6

This recipe comes from Chris's close friend and bandmate, Christopher Bear. When they're on tour, Chris and Christopher throw barbecues next to the bus as often as possible. With only two portable hibachi grills and a knife at their disposal, simplicity is key—and crowd-pleasing is pretty crucial. The secret to this recipe is that the cabbage is marinated and then grilled, which gives it even more flavor. It's fantastic on a burger or as a side for any BBQ on any day of summer.

---

1 cup sesame oil

1¼ cups rice wine vinegar

¾ cup tamari soy sauce

1 4-inch piece of peeled fresh ginger, minced

4 garlic cloves, minced

1 medium head of red cabbage

2 handfuls of fresh cilantro, chopped

In a large bowl, mix together the oil, vinegar, soy sauce, ginger, and garlic. Trim the root of the cabbage, quarter it, and put in a large bowl. (If it's very large, then cut into 6 wedges.) Pour the oil mixture over the cabbage wedges and let it marinate for at least 1 hour at room temperature.

Preheat a grill until very hot. Remove the cabbage wedges and tap against the bowl to shake off the marinade. Throw the cabbage down on the grill, avoiding the center (the hottest part of the grill) and reserve the marinade to use as a dressing for after the cabbage is cooked. Close the lid of the grill and allow the cabbage to roast. After about 7 minutes, flip the pieces, cover, and cook for another 7 minutes. Now move the wedges to the center of the grill to blacken, turning every couple of minutes so it doesn't burn to a crisp.

The outermost leaves will naturally start peeling away, so keep pulling them off until all the layers have seared and blackened slightly. Chop all the cabbage into thin strips, toss with the dressing to taste, add cilantro, and serve.

THE HAMBURGER

SERVES 6

We considered it our personal duty to perfect the method of making an amazing burger. Although it's not that complicated, it does take a little finesse to get a final product that's really, really good.

We're not purists—we like a hit of flavor in the meat mixture, and one ingredient we find key is a healthy amount of onions. They add punch to the flavor of the meat and help keep the burger extra juicy and delicious. Another tip is to cut your onions and garlic as small as possible so that the flavor folds in seamlessly with no detectable chunks. But most importantly, you want to taste your burger before it even hits the grill. It's just like beef tartare. So after everything's mixed, take a taste. See what it needs. It should be delicious before it's even cooked. Our final piece of advice is to salt just the surface of the patties right before they're grilled. That way the salt pulls the moisture only out of the surface of the meat, which helps it get a nice crust on the outside without drying out the inside. But the most important thing about burger cooking is that it should feel fun and easy. If you're nervous about your burger-making skills, don't fret: Just give people more beer.

2 pounds ground beef with an 80:20 fat ratio

1 large yellow or sweet onion, minced

2 garlic cloves, minced

1 to 2 jalapeño peppers, seeded and minced

3 tablespoons bourbon

3 tablespoons Worcestershire sauce

1 cup finely chopped fresh parsley

1 tablespoon freshly ground black pepper

Grapeseed or vegetable oil

1 tablespoon kosher salt

6 buns

Tomatoes, onions, mayonnaise, pickles, or other toppings of your choice (the Grilled Red Cabbage Slaw on page 197 is great)

(recipe continues)

In a bowl, combine the beef, onion, garlic, and jalapeño with the bourbon and Worcestershire sauce. (Depending on how much spice you want, you can use more or less jalapeño. Also, leaving in the seeds will add even more heat. You can always add more later when you adjust the seasoning.) Let this mixture marinate while you prep other items for your meal—it only gets better as it sits. So this is a great time to get your grill nice and smoking hot and clean.

Add the parsley and pepper to the meat mixture and combine well. Try a pinch of the meat and adjust the seasoning to taste. (If you're nervous about tasting the meat raw, grill a small bite of it and taste that.) When you're happy, divide the meat into 6 balls, and gently form them into patties.

Once the grill is very hot, use your grill brush to scour off any bits from the grate. Roll up a dish towel, coat it lightly with oil, and rub it along the grate so your food doesn't stick. Now you're ready to throw the burgers down. Salt the side of the meat that is about to meet the flames. Place the patties salt side down on the grill and let cook for 4 minutes with the lid open. After 4 minutes, salt the tops of the burger, and flip the patties over. Continue to cook for another 3 to 5 minutes or until they are done to your preference. You can tell by just touching a patty. If it gives easily and is soft, it's still rare. Once you feel a little resistance, it's medium-rare. Firmer than that is getting into medium and then well-done territory.

Grill up some buns and layer the patties with your toppings of choice.

TAL'S POTATO SALAD

SERVES 6

This potato salad is a barbecue classic that Tal, Ithai's brother, has made a staple out of. We're not sure he's invited anywhere anymore unless he shows up with it. Instead of mayo, he uses a mustard vinaigrette plus a few soft-boiled eggs to give it creamy body with complex flavor. Try to buy organic potatoes whenever possible; because potatoes and other root vegetables absorb everything that is put into the soil, you'll want to make sure they're not absorbing chemicals you don't want to eat.

---

18 small new potatoes—red, yellow, purple, doesn't matter

⅔ pound green beans or haricots verts

6 large eggs

1 medium red onion, diced, or 1 bunch of scallions (white and green parts), chopped

1 bunch of fresh dill, or to taste, chopped

3 tablespoons Dijon mustard

1 garlic clove, minced

6 to 9 tablespoons red wine vinegar

6 to 9 tablespoons olive oil

Salt and freshly ground black pepper

⅓ cup bread crumbs

Cover the potatoes with cold, generously salted water in a large saucepan and bring to a boil. Reduce to a simmer and cook until they can be easily pierced with a cake tester, about 20 minutes. Remove from the water and set aside to cool (throwing them in the fridge is fine).

Fill a bowl with ice and water. Bring the water in the saucepan back up to a boil and add the green beans. Blanch for 1 to 2 minutes, until bright green and crisp-tender. Remove the green beans and chill in the ice bath.

Bring the water back up to a boil and carefully add the eggs. Let cook at a rolling boil for 5 minutes. Transfer the eggs to the ice bath. Once cool enough to handle, gently crack the shells and peel. (This is a great task for a friend in need of a job in the kitchen.)

Slice the potatoes about ¼ inch thick. Halve the beans lengthwise and cut into 1-inch pieces.

In a mixing bowl, combine the potatoes, green beans, onion, and dill.

Make a vinaigrette by combining the mustard, garlic, vinegar, and oil in a mason jar. Give it a shake and season with salt and pepper.

Crush the soft-boiled eggs into the potato–green bean mixture with some dressing. Adjust with more salt or dressing, to taste. You can serve immediately, but it's best after an hour in the fridge.

TOMATO SEASON

There comes a point in the summer when the farmers' markets are exploding with tomatoes. These peak-season gems are nothing like the sad-looking, mealy beefsteaks that sit in the grocery store the rest of the year. They're sweet and juicy and fragrant and don't need a single drop of oil or salt to taste amazing. If it's late summer and we're eating, chances are there's a tomato on the plate. Our Israeli-Style Tomato Cucumber Salad (page 218) and Tomato and Sweet Corn Salad (page 247) are two great summer staples, and here are a few others to get you inspired.

RED SAUCE

MAKES 3 QUARTS

There are variations on the basic red sauce method in kitchens all over the world, including ours. This one in particular works well any time of year, as tomatoes aren't always in season, even if we wish they were.

---

8 to 10 pounds plum tomatoes (about 40 tomatoes)

Extra-virgin olive oil

1½ large yellow onions, finely diced

2 heads of garlic

4 medium carrots, juiced or grated

Crushed red pepper flakes

Salt

2 bay leaves

8 sprigs fresh thyme

2 sprigs fresh oregano

8 whole black peppercorns, toasted

1 or 2 handfuls of basil, depending on how herbaceous you like it, chiffonade (see page 255)

NOTE: CANNED TOMATOES

If you don't get around to preserving summer tomatoes and want to make this dish in the winter, use jarred, not canned, tomatoes. We don't feel so good about cooking with canned goods because they can contain bisphenol-A (BPA), a toxic industrial chemical used for lining cans. We won't get into the gnarly details, but it's just not good for you. Plus, food sitting in a metal container for a long time tends to taste a bit like, well, metal.

Bring a large pot of water to a boil over high heat, salt the water, and fill a large bowl with ice water.

With the tip of your knife, make a small *X* on the bottom of each tomato. Add a few tomatoes at a time to the hot water and allow them to boil for 20 seconds, or until you see the skin starting to peel away from the flesh. Transfer to the ice water. After a few seconds they should be cool enough to handle and the skins should slip off easily when pulled. If not, put the tomatoes back into the boiling water for 10 seconds more and shock again with ice water. Peel all the tomatoes using this method.

Put the tomatoes in a large bowl and crush them with your hands. Remove the cores.

(recipe continues)

Generously coat the bottom of a large, heavy-bottomed stockpot with olive oil and heat over medium-low heat. Add the onions, 3 whole cloves of garlic, and grated carrots (if not using juice) and very gently sweat them until they are translucent and sweet, about 5 minutes. Once the onions are soft and translucent, add 1 tablespoon of red pepper flakes and a few pinches of salt. If you've juiced the carrots, pour that in now. Let the mixture cook gently for another 2 to 3 minutes.

Add the tomatoes to the pot along with a tied cheesecloth pouch filled with the remaining garlic (just cut the heads in half, exposing the cloves), bay leaf, thyme, oregano, and peppercorns.

Turn the heat up to high, bring the pot to a boil, then reduce to a simmer. Let the sauce cook for a good 4 hours, occasionally stirring and scraping down the sides with a spatula to prevent it from burning and also to put all that good flavor back into the sauce. You're looking for the sauce to cook down to a thick consistency. When it is done, remove the cheesecloth pouch and discard.

We like a big rustic red sauce, but if you want a smooth sauce, wait until the sauce has cooled a bit, and blend it in a blender or with a handheld immersion blender.

Eat as much as you want or can handle, pack the rest into containers, and freeze them to last you for months.

CHRIS'S SLOW-ROASTED TOMATO SAUCE

MAKES ABOUT 3 QUARTS

This recipe is inspired by Chris's friend Jacopo's grandmother from northern Italy. She roasts her tomatoes in the hot summer sun, which deepens their flavor and yields the best red sauce he's ever tasted. You can get the same effect using a low oven.

---

8 to 10 pounds fresh San Marzano, plum, or small heirloom tomatoes, halved lengthwise

Salt

Extra-virgin olive oil

5 whole garlic cloves, plus 3 garlic cloves, minced

4 sprigs fresh rosemary

10 fresh basil leaves, finely chopped

Preheat the oven to 200°F or the lowest temperature your oven will go.

Arrange the tomatoes on rimmed baking sheets, cut side up. Top them with a dusting of salt, a drizzle of oil, the rosemary, and the whole garlic cloves. Roast for 6 hours, or until they completely soften and turn deep red.

Discard the rosemary and whole garlic cloves and transfer the tomatoes to a large saucepot over medium heat. Bring to a simmer. Add the minced garlic. Cook for a few minutes so the garlic incorporates; if the sauce is watery, cook until it's thick. Season with salt. Stir in the basil before serving. Pack extra sauce into containers and freeze; they will keep for months.

THE PERFECT BLT

MAKES 2 SANDWICHES

There's nothing like a good BLT, and certainly nothing easier to make. The real key—like any recipe—is to use the best possible ingredients, especially the tomatoes. We prefer heirloom, but any variety in season will do. As for bacon, treat yourself to quality, thick-cut slices and not thin, little strips that have been sitting in plastic their entire lifetime. And if you really want to get serious about taking this to another level, consider making your own mayonnaise, too.

---

3 thick slices of high-quality slab bacon

1 heirloom tomato

Salt

Extra-virgin olive oil, as needed

4 slices of pumpernickel or sourdough bread

Chris's Homemade Mayo (recipe follows) or good-quality store-bought mayonnaise

1 handful of fresh basil leaves or arugula

Halve the bacon lengthwise and cook it in a large cast-iron skillet over medium heat until rendered and crisped to your liking. Drain the bacon slices on paper towels and save the fat for another use. Slice the tomato into wide disks. Don't be dainty—a fresh tomato can hold its own in this sandwich—and salt the tomato slices. Add enough oil to the pan to coat, set back over medium heat, and toast the bread on one side until lightly browned. Slather with mayonnaise on the untoasted side and top with the bacon, tomato, and basil.

CHRIS'S HOMEMADE MAYO

MAKES ¾ CUP

At one point in my life I was determined to master making mayo at home. For about a week I'd get home after a long day at the studio and practice, hoping to find the best way to make this classic recipe. I didn't have a blender at the time, only a whisk. So while I can attest that you can do this with no fancy equipment, it's a lot easier if you have a blender or food processor.

---

1 large egg yolk

½ teaspoon Dijon mustard

1 teaspoon white wine vinegar

1½ teaspoons fresh lemon juice, plus more to taste

½ teaspoon sea salt

¾ cup sunflower or extra-virgin olive oil

In a blender or bowl, combine the egg yolk, mustard, vinegar, 1½ teaspoons of the lemon juice, the salt, and ¼ cup of the oil. Blend or whisk vigorously until the ingredients have come together. Then, while still blending or whisking, slowly stream in the rest of the oil, a few drops at a time, until the mixture is completely emulsified. Emulsification, by definition, is combining two liquids that wouldn't otherwise combine without a little coaxing. To coax this mayo to come together, the secret is taking your time when adding the oil. Once the mixture is thick and mayo-like in consistency, taste and adjust the seasoning with more lemon juice or salt if desired. Store in an airtight container in the fridge for about 1 week.

ITHAI'S SHAKSHUKA

SERVES 1 TO 2

Growing up, most of my family lived in Israel and my best memories all revolve around the food—whether it was the sunflower seeds we always grabbed at the store on the corner or the plate of hummus that's sold on almost every street. And then there's shakshuka, a hearty breakfast stew of slow-cooked tomatoes, garlic, and spices like paprika and za'atar, a sort of Mediterranean herbes de Provence, all topped off with—my favorite—an egg. It's a one-pot meal that is easy enough to make while half asleep in the morning and even easier if you have some of our Red Sauce (page 204) on hand. But above all, Mediterranean food has a way of being fresh and clean while still giving you a good, filling start to the day. It's best served with a piece of toast and, obviously, a good cup of coffee.

Extra-virgin olive oil

¼ white onion, diced

1 garlic clove, minced

Salt

1 cup Red Sauce (page 204) or good tomato sauce

3 large eggs

Freshly ground black pepper

Pinch of paprika

Pinch of za'atar

Pinch of chopped fresh parsley

Add enough oil to a medium cast-iron skillet to coat the bottom and heat over a medium flame. Add the onion and garlic and allow them to sweat with a pinch of salt. Once translucent, add the red sauce. Raise the heat so the sauce comes to a boil, then reduce to a simmer.

Break the eggs over the pan and season with salt and pepper. Add the paprika and za'atar. Be careful with the paprika and za'atar—they can be overpowering if used too heavily, and you can always add more later. Cook the egg-sauce mixture over low heat until the eggs are cooked to your liking. I personally prefer them to be on the runny side. Consider that the eggs will continue cooking even after the heat's turned off, so cook them just a hair under how you like them, but be sure the white is all opaque when you turn off the heat.

Finish with the parsley and serve the whole thing still in the pan with toast and coffee.

DINNER 17

Slow-Roasted Eggplant Crostini

───────────

Seared Scallops with Fresh Corn Andouille "Grits"

───────────

Israeli-Style Tomato Cucumber Salad
with Fried Soft-Boiled Egg

WHAT TO DRINK

Vinho Verde or a light sparkling red, such as Lambrusco

SLOW-ROASTED EGGPLANT CROSTINI

SERVES 8

This is a perfect example of how good eggplant can get when it's cooked low and slow. It not only takes on a sweeter taste, but it also keeps its beautiful color. If you can, make this a day in advance and store it in the fridge to let the flavors blend.

---

2 large eggplants

1 head of garlic

Extra-virgin olive oil

1 baguette or caraway-seeded bread, cut into ¾-inch slices and toasted

1 red onion, chopped fine

1 teaspoon honey, or to taste

2 pinches of ground cumin

Paprika (optional)

Pinch of lemon zest (optional)

Salt and freshly ground black pepper

¼ cup roughly chopped fresh parsley

Toasted pine nuts (see page 255; optional)

Fresh lemon juice (optional)

Preheat the oven to 325°F.

Set the eggplants on your stove's grates over a high flame (or use your broiler), turning once you get a good char. Once charred on all sides, transfer the eggplants to a cooling rack set inside a rimmed baking sheet and put in the oven. Roast until a cake tester glides in easily with no resistance, 45 minutes to 1 hour. While the eggplant is roasting, slice the head of garlic in half widthwise, coat in oil, then wrap in a little foil pouch. Put it in the oven and roast alongside the eggplant. Cook until a cake tester can easily pierce the cloves, 45 minutes to 1 hour.

Remove the garlic and eggplant from the oven, cut each eggplant in half, and cool to room temperature.

Scoop out the eggplant's flesh onto a cutting board. Give it a rough chop. You don't want it to be completely mushy. Transfer it to a bowl.

Squeeze out the cloves of roasted garlic onto the cutting board and use the side of your knife to smash it into a paste. Fold the garlic into the eggplant, tasting after each addition (2 to 3 cloves should be plenty; save the extra for another use). Stir in the onion, honey, cumin, paprika (if using), and lemon zest (if using). Add salt and pepper to taste.

Stir in a bit of oil until you've reached a dip-like thickness that can hold its shape when spooned over bread. Spread on toasted bread and top with parsley, and if you want, pine nuts and lemon juice.

SEARED SCALLOPS
WITH FRESH CORN ANDOUILLE "GRITS"

SERVES 4

It might not look like it a first glance, but this dish pulls its inspiration from the classic shrimp-and-grits combination, but instead of using ground dried corn (grits), we're using whole kernels of fresh sweet corn and adding some Andouille sausage to give it a kick. Then there's the herbaceous sauce. We're calling it a "chimiverde"—a cross between chimichurri and salsa verde, two olive oil–based, herb-forward sauces. It goes with everything, and the vinegary brightness makes it great with meat and fish.

---

2 ears of fresh corn

Grapeseed or vegetable oil

1 small shallot, diced

1 garlic clove, minced

1 link of Andouille sausage, cut into ¼-inch disks

Salt and freshly ground black pepper, to taste

About 1½ tablespoons unsalted butter

12 large sea scallops (about ¾ pound) (see Note)

Wondra flour

2 garlic cloves, smashed

Chimiverde Sauce (recipe follows)

1 lime wedge

½ cup chopped fresh parsley

½ cup chopped fresh mint

Shuck the corn by peeling off its tough outer leaves and peeling off the silk sticking to the kernels. (Doing this under running water works well.) Stand each ear vertically on your cutting board and run your knife down its length, cutting where the kernels hit the cob. Collect the kernels in a bowl.

In a medium saucepan, add enough oil to coat the bottom and heat over a medium-low flame. Sweat the shallot, minced garlic, and sausage until the shallot is translucent, 5 to 6 minutes. Season with salt and pepper and add the corn.

Continue to sweat over low heat for another 5 minutes. The corn will go from pale to vibrant yellow. At this point, add salt to taste and a teaspoon of butter. Gently toss the corn mixture until evenly coated with butter, then move the pan to the back of your range.

Get a cast-iron or heavy-bottomed skillet hot over a medium-high flame, then add enough oil to coat the bottom. While you wait for the pan to heat, dredge the scallops with Wondra.

(recipe continues)

When the oil is shimmering, carefully place the scallops in the skillet, and season with salt. You should hear a faint sizzle as they are cooking. Allow the scallops to sit in the pan undisturbed for about 4 minutes.

Once a golden crust has formed—you'll be able to see it creeping up the side of the scallops—throw in a generous tablespoon of butter and the smashed garlic. Allow the butter to foam, then flip each scallop and baste with the butter for 30 seconds to a minute. Remove them from the pan and serve immediately over the corn.

To finish the dish, add a touch of chimiverde (you don't want it to overpower the scallops), a squeeze of lime, the parsley, and the mint.

NOTE: BUYING SCALLOPS
When purchasing scallops, check that they are "dry," or "undipped," that is, untreated with sodium tripolyphosphate, which makes them absorb water and impossible to sear.

CHIMIVERDE SAUCE

MAKES 2 CUPS

This recipe makes about 2 cups, much more than you'll need for this dish, but you can keep the extra sauce in your fridge for a week and put it on everything from salads to steaks.

½ cup chopped white onion

2 garlic cloves

¼ cup chopped fresh parsley

¼ cup chopped fresh mint

1 tomatillo, charred (on the grill or over your stovetop burners)

1 red chile pepper, chopped

2 teaspoons fresh oregano

1 teaspoon fresh thyme

⅓ cup Chardonnay vinegar

1 anchovy fillet

1 teaspoon capers

1 good pinch of paprika

¾ cup olive oil

Grated zest of 2 limes

Salt and freshly ground black pepper

Place the onion, garlic, parsley, mint, tomatillo, chile, oregano, thyme, vinegar, anchovy, capers, and paprika in a blender. Pulse until well combined but not completely smooth, more like a salsa than a vinaigrette. Transfer to a bowl and add the oil and lime zest. Taste and season with salt and pepper, if necessary. At this point, you can store the sauce in the fridge, but make sure it's back to room temperature before adding it to the scallops (or any other hot dish, for that matter).

ISRAELI-STYLE TOMATO CUCUMBER SALAD
WITH FRIED SOFT-BOILED EGG
SERVES 4

At just about any restaurant in Israel you can get a salad that's almost always the same thing: cucumber, tomato, parsley, and half a lemon on the side. It is like a universal language there. So not surprisingly, Ithai's parents served this to him all the time when he was growing up. His favorite part was when he and his brother would dip bread in the leftover dressing. It's why we've added a breaded egg to the mix—it not only adds a bit of something both crunchy and soft, but it will also soak up all the flavorful juices from the salad. Because the dish is so straightforward, it's crucial that you find the freshest produce possible.

---

3 large ripe tomatoes

4 Kirby cucumbers

1 red onion

½ cup finely chopped fresh parsley

Salt and freshly ground black pepper

1 tablespoon Dijon mustard

1 teaspoon honey

¼ garlic clove, grated or minced

Juice of 1 lemon

¼ cup plus 1 tablespoon good-quality extra-virgin olive oil

6 large eggs

Canola oil

All-purpose flour

1½ cups panko bread crumbs

Dice the tomatoes and cucumbers, making the pieces all roughly the same size. Thinly slice the onion. Combine the tomatoes, cucumbers, and onions in a large bowl, add a handful of parsley, and toss. Season with salt and pepper to taste.

In a mason jar, combine the mustard, honey, garlic, and a couple grinds of pepper. Add the lemon juice and olive oil, then give the jar a good shake until the dressing emulsifies.

In a large saucepan, bring enough water to cover the eggs by an inch to a rolling boil. Fill a large bowl with room-temperature water. Gently lower 4 of the eggs into the boiling water and cook for 4 minutes and 45 seconds. Transfer the cooked eggs to the water bath to cool, then carefully peel them, set them back in the water bath, and reserve.

Fill a large saucepan with 3 inches of canola oil, making sure you have at least 2 inches of clearance. Heat the oil over medium-high heat to 375°F. If you don't have a candy thermometer to test the temperature, throw in a few bread crumbs. If they sizzle immediately, the oil is ready.

While the oil is heating, set up a dredging station. Fill 1 small bowl with flour and season it with salt. In another small bowl, beat the remaining 2 eggs. Pour the panko into a third small bowl.

Once the oil is at temperature, remove the eggs—one at a time—from the water bath and carefully dry with towels. Dip each egg first in the flour bowl, then in the beaten egg, and then the panko, making sure to lightly but evenly coat at each stage.

Working in 2 batches, carefully lower the dredged eggs into the oil and fry until just golden brown. Remove the eggs and set them aside on a paper-towel-lined plate. Season with salt.

Toss the tomato-cucumber mixture with enough dressing to coat and season with salt and pepper—this salad can take on more seasoning than you think. Portion out as desired and top each plate or bowl with a fried soft-boiled egg.

DINNER 18

**Lavender–Goat Cheese Crostini
with Peaches and Mint**

Fire-Roasted Trout with Grilled Figs

**Quinoa Salad
with Grapes and Hazelnuts**

Berry–Blood Orange Trifles

WHAT TO DRINK

Sunset Spot

A rich, white wine with acidity,
such as a Spanish white like Godello,
or an Alsatian white such as Grüner Veltliner

SUNSET SPOT

MAKES 1 COCKTAIL

During the summer evenings, once the magic hour approaches, we all head down the road from our house, cross train tracks to the shore of the Hudson River and wait for the sun to go down. The colors of the sky, the shadows of the Catskill Mountains shimmering and reflecting off the river—the view is breathtaking. This drink not only complements the mood of the hour—warm sunset, cooling air—but also some of the colors that make it so extraordinary.
—*Nino*

---

1 or 2 thin slices peeled fresh ginger

2 to 3 dashes of Angostura bitters

Sugar cube (optional)

½ ounce fresh lime juice

1½ ounces Del Maguey Vida mescal

2 to 3 thin slices plum

Club soda

In a mixing glass or shaker, cover the ginger with the Angostura bitters and muddle. If you want a sweeter drink, add a sugar cube before muddling. Add lime juice and mescal. Shake with ice and strain into a Collins glass filled with ice. Add the plum and top with club soda.

LAVENDER–GOAT CHEESE CROSTINI
WITH PEACHES AND MINT

SERVES 4

We came up with this idea when asked to throw together a lunch for a large group of people one summer afternoon. We wanted a nice, light summer snack that would taste as good as it sounded.

½ cup honey

A pinch of lavender, fresh or dried

2 peaches

½ baguette, cut into 1-inch slices, toasted

½ pound goat cheese, young, aged in ash—whichever you like

Fresh mint leaves, chiffonade (see page 255)

In a small pan, warm the honey and lavender over low heat for about 4 minutes. Remove from the heat and allow the honey to cool down until it is just warmer than room temperature.

Slice the peaches into small wedges, about ¼ inch thick.

Top the toasts with a good amount of goat cheese, followed by a couple of peach slices. Add a few strings of mint, then lightly drizzle everything with the lavender-honey mixture.

FIRE-ROASTED TROUT
WITH GRILLED FIGS

SERVES 4

Trout is one of our favorite fishes because fortunately it can be caught wild in most of America. That means it is easily accessible, whether you're fishing for your own or picking up one at your fish market. Plus its flavor is sweet, rich, and mild, and it's usually just the right size for dinner.

For this preparation, we use a grill grate set over an open fire to cook the fish, which gives it some smoky character. We highly recommend breaking this out at your next cookout, but since you won't always have the option of a fire pit or grill, feel free to treat this as if it were a piece of meat, searing the fish in a pan and finishing in the oven, as described in our meat-searing method (see page 253). Either way, this dish takes less than ten minutes from start to finish once you have your fire or grill going.

½ cup hazelnuts (optional)

12 fresh figs

Grapeseed or vegetable oil

4 whole trout (about 1 pound each), cleaned and butterflied (ask your fishmonger to do this for you)

Extra-virgin olive oil

8 to 12 sprigs of fresh thyme

4 bay leaves

Salt

2 tablespoons balsamic vinegar

A few handfuls of microgreens (see Note)

1 lemon, cut into wedges

Coarse sea salt

Good-quality extra-virgin olive oil, for finishing

NOTE: MICROGREENS

It used to be you'd only see these on restaurant menus, but now a lot of markets and stores are carrying microgreens—or lettuces and vegetables that are harvested at the seedling stage. There are all different kinds—micro-arugula, -basil, and -kale, to name a few—and they're great as the base of a salad or for adding some green and delicate flavor to a dish. If you can't find them, feel free to use any small lettuce, like baby arugula, or lettuce made smaller, *like chopped radicchio.*

Prepare your fire and set up your grill. Allow the fire to get really hot—and the grill to get completely cleaned from the heat of the fire—then wait for it to burn down enough so it's a bed of hellfire-hot coals.

Toast the nuts, if using them: When your fire is ready, set a small saucepan over the grill grate—or medium flame if using your stovetop—and allow to heat. Toss in the hazelnuts

(recipe continues)

ula and finish for 2 minutes on the other side, or until the fish is just cooked through. While the fish cooks, return the small saucepan to the grate or directly in the coals. Add the balsamic vinegar and let reduce by half. Reserve.

When the fish is done, remove it from the grill and let it cool for 3 minutes on a warm plate. Meanwhile, roll the figs around with a spoon so they don't overcook on one side. Test them for doneness by piercing with a cake tester, then holding it to your lip. It should feel warm. Remove the figs and toss them in a bowl with the reduced balsamic vinegar while still hot. Set aside.

Once the fish has rested, fillet to serve: Place the fish on a cutting board. Remove the head and tail. Then, keeping your knife parallel to your cutting board, cut along the spine. (It may be easier to use a dinner knife to fillet the fish, so you don't cut through the spine with your sharp kitchen knife.) You should be able to (carefully) lift the fillet away from the rib cage with a spatula or spoon. Then lift the spine from the bottom fillet.

To serve, make a bed of microgreens on each plate and top with a few figs. Lay a trout fillet on top of the figs and finish each with a generous squeeze of lemon, a sprinkle of coarse sea salt, the hazelnuts (if using), and finishing oil.

and let them toast, rolling them around a bit until they are lightly browned and fragrant. Remove them from the pan and set aside.

Coat the figs with grapeseed oil. Coat the fish with a small amount of olive oil, both on the outside and inside the cavity. Stuff each fish with 2 to 3 sprigs of thyme, 1 bay leaf, and a pinch of salt; then lightly salt the outside. Arrange the fish and the figs on the grill, leaving enough room to flip the fish over when the time comes. Cook the trout for 3 minutes on the first side, then flip over with a thin spat-

QUINOA SALAD
WITH GRAPES AND HAZELNUTS
SERVES 4

It took us a bit to come around to quinoa—it seemed like a food that you'd make yourself buy in a health food store rather than something tasty you'd look forward to eating. However, as we began to see more of our friends eating it, we began to look for ways to make it interesting, and it's actually a really versatile ingredient that takes on flavor really well. Plus, it also happens to be high in protein and is one of the healthiest grains out there. This version goes well with just about any fish. The fresh grapes and toasted hazelnuts make the salad crunchy, juicy, and delicious.

---

1 cup quinoa (any variety)

2 cups vegetable stock

Salt

1 bay leaf (optional)

2 to 4 garlic cloves (optional)

2 sprigs fresh thyme (optional)

16 seedless green and red grapes, quartered

¼ cup toasted hazelnuts, crushed

1 tablespoon honey

¼ cup champagne vinegar

2 tablespoons extra-virgin olive oil

3 fresh basil leaves, finely chopped

4 fresh mint leaves, finely chopped

½ bunch of fresh parsley, finely chopped

Grated zest of 1 lemon

Grated zest of ½ orange

Freshly ground black pepper

In a fine-mesh sieve, rinse the quinoa well until the water runs clear and there aren't any more "suds." Drain and transfer to a medium saucepan. Add the stock, a pinch of salt, the bay leaf (if using), garlic (if using), and/or thyme (if using) and bring to a boil over medium-high heat. Cover, reduce heat to low, and simmer until the liquid is absorbed, about 15 minutes. Keep the pot covered but remove it from the heat and let sit for 5 minutes. Remove the lid and fluff the quinoa with a fork, taking out any aromatics you added earlier.

Transfer the quinoa to a bowl and fold in the grapes and hazelnuts. Then stir in the honey, vinegar, and oil. Add in the basil, mint, parsley, lemon zest, and orange zest and toss everything together. Season with salt and pepper to taste, and serve warm or let cool to room temperature.

BERRY–BLOOD ORANGE TRIFLES

SERVES 8

With their vibrant layers of fruit, custard, and ladyfingers, these trifles are beautiful. You can try and find some individual vintage glasses to serve them in or find one large glass bowl that could be a table feature. It's always better to make and assemble this dessert the day before so it has time to set and take on all the flavors.

---

3 large eggs

3 large egg yolks

½ cup plus 2 tablespoons sugar

5 cups heavy cream

1 vanilla bean, split open, seeds scraped out and reserved

1 packet ladyfinger cookies, such as Savoiardi

2 cups dry sherry

3 blood oranges

1 quart mixed berries such as blackberries, raspberries, currants, and blueberries

1 cup pecan halves or any nut of your choice, toasted (see page 255)

In a large mixing bowl, combine the eggs, egg yolks, and sugar and whisk just to combine. (Don't leave sugar on the yolks without mixing, as the sugar "cooks" the eggs, leaving you with hard lumps in your custard.) Set aside.

In a medium saucepan over medium-low heat, bring 3½ cups of the cream, the vanilla seeds, and vanilla pod to a boil. Remove from the heat and slowly pour the cream over the egg mixture while whisking. Then add the egg and cream mixture back to the pan and place over very low heat. Stir constantly, scraping the bottom of the pan with a heatproof rubber spatula, to thicken the custard. (If the heat is too high, the mixture will scramble.)

Use a candy thermometer to gauge its progress. Once the custard has reached 156°F, remove it from the stove, remove and discard the vanilla pod, and pass the custard through a fine-mesh sieve into a bowl. Cover the surface with plastic wrap (which will keep a skin from forming on top) and leave in the fridge to cool.

While the custard is cooling, set out 8 glasses. Break up the cookies into small pieces, but not a fine crumble, and place one cookie's worth of pieces at the bottom of each glass. Top the cookie pieces with ¼ cup sherry so that they soak up the liquid and become soft. Set aside.

Supreme the oranges (see page 41).

Divide the berries and oranges among the glasses and top with the chilled custard. When ready to serve, whip the remaining 1½ cups cream to soft peaks. To finish, top each trifle with whipped cream and pecans.

SMOKED TROUT PÂTÉ

MAKES 2 CUPS

When we were hanging out at our friend Dan's house a couple years back, he kept giving us pieces of what was arguably the best smoked trout we'd ever had. He said his neighbor Lenny made it. Sure enough, just down the road was a little store in the back of Lenny's house where his mother sold his smoked trout. Well, it wasn't so much a store as it was a mudroom that they just happened to sell trout and honey out of.

It seemed necessary to figure out a way to work in a smoked trout recipe, even if it's as simple as making it into a spread that you can throw on some toast. Smoked trout in general is pretty delicious, so it doesn't necessarily have to be Lenny's. But if you live near Fort Greene, Brooklyn, and can make it to the farmers' market, it's worth checking his out.

½ pound smoked trout, flaked into bite-size pieces

½ cup crème fraîche

¼ cup olive oil

Juice of 1 lemon

1 scallion, white and green parts, sliced

1 fresh or dried fig, cut into ¼-inch dice

1 small red chile pepper, chopped

¼ cup chopped fresh parsley

1 tablespoon pickled mustard seeds (see page 196)

1 clove roasted garlic (optional, but if you have it around, it can't hurt)

Salt and freshly ground black pepper

In a medium bowl, combine the trout, crème fraîche, oil, lemon juice, scallion, fig, chile, parsley, mustard seeds, and garlic (if using) and fold to make a diplike consistency. Add salt and pepper to taste. Spread over a piece of toast with a bit of avocado and you're good to go.

DINNER 19

The Cheese Plate

Chris's Gruyère Pastry

Fig–Earl Grey Jam

WHAT TO DRINK

A white Rancio or Muscat de Rivesaltes or a dry,
earthy sparkling red, such as Lambrusco

THE CHEESE PLATE

Sometimes there are nights when you just don't feel like cooking a dinner. When that happens, you need to say, "Forget it," and make yourself a cheese plate. Usually we try to assemble one out of whatever's in the fridge, but if you're heading to the store, think about getting a variety of cheeses.

Generally speaking, we dig getting a bleu cheese, then both a hard and soft cheese. From there, we'll go with one cow's milk and one goat's milk, just to mix it up. Then all you have to do is toss in some charcuterie, olives, roasted garlic, ripe figs or berries (if in season), and small toasts or crackers. But if you are in a cooking mood and want to make this a truly ultimate cheese plate, then go for Chris's Gruyère Pastry (page 234) and Fig–Earl Grey Jam (page 235).

Just be sure to give your cheeses some time to warm up at room temperature. When they're cold, you won't get to appreciate their full flavor. Soft cheeses in particular need that extra love to get back to their natural gooey texture.

CHRIS'S GRUYÈRE PASTRY

SERVES 6

Almost every holiday, Chris's mom would ask him to make this, because it requires some intense stirring for about 20 minutes. You'll see once you make this recipe that it's a good job to pass off to a friend who needs a good workout. Aside from building strong arms, though, this is a delicious buttery pastry that has a flaky croissant-like texture combined with the richness of Gruyère. How could it *not* be good? Plus, it's nearly impossible to mess up. If you're looking to step up your cheese plate game, this is a perfect addition.

---

8 tablespoons (1 stick) unsalted butter, plus more for greasing the pan

1 cup all-purpose flour

4 large eggs

1½ cups grated Gruyère cheese

1 teaspoon Dijon mustard

1 teaspoon salt

½ teaspoon ground mustard seed

Preheat the oven to 450°F.

In a medium saucepan, combine the butter with 1 cup water and bring to a rolling boil over medium-high heat. Make sure the butter completely melts. Reduce the heat to medium-low, add in the flour, and stir vigorously with a wooden spoon until the mixture forms a ball and comes away from the sides of the pan, about 20 minutes. Remove from the heat.

Add the eggs one at a time, stirring until each egg has been completely incorporated before adding the next. The dough will be smooth and shiny. Stir in the Gruyère, Dijon mustard, salt, and mustard seed.

On a buttered baking sheet, form a ring of roughly 1½-inch-round dollops that is 9 inches in diameter with half of the dough. Make a second ring layered directly on top of the first with the remaining dough. (This gives the pastry a lighter, flakier texture.)

Bake for 10 minutes, then reduce the oven temperature to 350°F. Bake for another 10 minutes. Reduce the temperature to 325°F and continue baking until the pastry is puffy and lightly browned, about 15 more minutes.

Remove from the oven and poke holes in the pastry with a fork to let steam out. Let the pastry cool on a wire rack, then cut into small wedges and serve.

FIG–EARL GREY JAM

MAKES 3 CUPS

This sweet, textural jam pairs really well with cheese, especially a sharp bleu or soft brie style. It's also great spooned over yogurt, granola, or toast. The Earl Grey leaves go directly in the jam instead of getting strained out, since they'll eventually soften and are completely edible. Just make sure to use a high-quality tea.

---

5 cups fresh figs, roughly chopped

2 tablespoons loose Earl Grey tea

3½ cups sugar

Juice of 1 lemon

Preheat the oven to 275°F.

Place a small plate in the fridge; you'll see why in a bit.

In a heavy-bottomed, medium saucepan, cook the figs over low heat with the tea until they start to collapse. Add the sugar, stir until combined, then stir in the lemon juice. Raise the heat to medium, let the mixture come to a boil, and cook until it is jamlike in texture. The old "plate in the fridge" test is good for seeing if it's done—jam that has reached its setting point (or 220°F) will "gel," or hold its shape, when dripped onto a cold plate. If the jam is still runny, let it boil for a few minutes more. When the jam gels, place it in containers with airtight lids. Let cool and store in the fridge for up to 2 weeks.

LILLIE'S TIPS FOR SUPERIOR JAMS
- *Don't leave your fruit lying around too long, especially berries. Buy ripe produce and use it quickly.*
- *Remember that jam is an ideal use of knobbly and misshapen—but perfectly delicious— fruit.*
- *The lemon juice is important because the tartness balances the sweetness of the jam and reacts with the fruit's natural pectins and sugars to help the jam set.*
- *When you're boiling the jam, don't stir it. The cold air will make it spit. Do stir every few minutes when it is cooling, to stop a skin from forming.*

DINNER 20

Turkish-Style Paella with Mussels,
Currants, and Mint

———

Whole Spit-Roasted Pig with Mustard Greens

———

Tomato and Sweet Corn Salad

———

Watermelon Grappa Granita

WHAT TO DRINK

Open Hydrant

———

A flavorful red like Malbec or Carménère from Chile
or the Loire Valley or Lambrusco, which is always a
great call on just about any summer day

TURKISH-STYLE PAELLA
WITH MUSSELS, CURRANTS, AND MINT
SERVES 8 TO 12 AS A SIDE

The inspiration for this dish came from the mussel snack carts set up at the fish markets in Turkey. At first it seemed strange to be selling shellfish as casual street food, but the locals seemed to be going nuts for it. As it turned out, the mussels, stuffed with pungently spiced seafood and rice, were out of this world. The sweet-savory balance of the currants and mint with the mussels and rice is really something. We've kept the same easy vibe of that dish here, but it stays in the skillet for an even simpler presentation—especially if you're making an enormous batch or two to feed a crowd. If you're making this with friends, we recommend handing off the mussel prep work.

---

1 pound mussels (about 20)

Grapeseed or vegetable oil

1 small white onion, diced

2 large garlic cloves, minced

1 red bird chile pepper, minced

Good pinch of herbes de Provence

Good pinch of ground turmeric

1 cup dry white wine

4½ cups seafood, chicken, or vegetable stock

3 cups long-grain rice

½ cup currants

Salt

Grated zest and juice of 1 lemon

1 small bunch of fresh mint, leaves roughly chopped

Sort through the mussels to make sure they are all alive. Do this by taking any open ones and squeezing them shut. If they're alive, they will stay closed on their own. Chuck those that do not. As for the ones that are already closed, keep them for now, but if they don't open after cooking them, they have to go, too.

Debeard the mussels by grabbing the little stringy beard sticking out from the opening of the shell. While holding the hinged end of the shell with one hand, pull the beard toward you, tugging it and the small white knobby bit attached to the end until they detach. Then give the mussel shells a scrub with a brush or scouring pad.

In a large stockpot over medium heat, heat enough oil to coat the bottom. Add the onion and garlic and sweat until soft, about 5 minutes. Add the chile, herbes de Provence, and turmeric. Reduce the heat to low, and let the ingredients cook together for about 20 minutes.

Pour in the wine to deglaze, making sure to loosen up any ingredients that have stuck to the bottom of the pan. Bring to a boil and then down to a simmer, cooking until the wine has reduced by half, about 5 minutes. Add your stock, return to a boil, and stir in your rice. Turn the heat down to a very gentle simmer, cover the pot, and cook for about 15 minutes, or until the rice has absorbed almost all the liquid.

Next, add your mussels. Cover the pot again and cook for another 7 to 10 minutes, or until all the mussels have fully opened. (Keep in mind that a few may never open, which means they didn't survive the journey and must be discarded.)

Once done, take the pot off the heat, stir in the currants, and taste the rice for seasoning. Add salt, if needed, and lemon zest, to taste. Just before serving, add the lemon juice and mint.

OPEN HYDRANT

MAKES 1 COCKTAIL

If you grew up in New York, then you know about open fire hydrants. Like an improvised water park in the middle of the asphalt street, the minute someone popped open the cap and the water started flowing, the whole block—kids, teens, adults—all found relief from the oppressive summer heat. I hope this drink brings just a little bit of that when sipped. —*Nino*

---

2 ounces Hendrick's gin

½ ounce fresh lime juice

¾ ounce cucumber juice

Good-quality tonic water

Freshly ground black pepper

Cucumber slices, for garnish

Shake the gin, lime juice, and cucumber juice with ice. Strain into a Collins glass filled with fresh ice. Top with the tonic water and a few grinds of pepper. Garnish with a slice of cucumber.

WHOLE SPIT-ROASTED PIG
WITH MUSTARD GREENS
SERVES A CROWD, ABOUT 40

We have always wanted to roast a whole pig over an open fire. It would be the perfect way to end summer—like a BBQ on steroids. More food, more friends, and more drinks, which equals more good times.

That said, this dinner is no joke. It was a massive challenge. But so what? It's the ultimate conquest. We had no idea if we'd be able to pull it off, but halfway through, when we realized it was going to work—that all that prep was paying off, that everyone was pulling together to make it happen, that this beautiful 35-pound pig was about to be dinner—there was nothing like that feeling. And we can honestly say that it was one of the best meals we've ever made.

---

1 pig (about 40 pounds), gutted and cleaned

6 pounds kosher salt, plus more as needed

3 pounds sugar, plus more as needed

2 bottles bourbon

4 heads of garlic, halved

1 4-ounce bottle of coriander seeds, toasted

1 4-ounce bottle of whole black peppercorns, toasted

10 bay leaves

Platza Oil (page 243)

4 pounds mustard greens or other tender braising greens, washed and chopped (see page 255)

Rice wine vinegar (optional)

5 quarts pickles, or so; use a variety, but watermelon rinds are perfect (optional)

Fireside Fruit Chutney (recipe follows)

SPECIAL EQUIPMENT

Roasting spit (see opposite)

50-gallon drum or large industrial garbage can or giant insulated cooler

Drum liner (like a massive 50-gallon garbage bag)

8 10-pound bags of ice

6 feet of wire

Good wire cutters

About 60 pieces of quartered, seasoned firewood, preferably cherry wood, but any fruit tree will do

Metal shovel

Long basting brush or long, thin twigs

1 to 2 large rimmed baking sheet trays with roasting racks that fit in them, depending on the size of the pig

A Week or Month Before the Roast

Find a pig of noble origins. It should be one that has been fed an organic diet and raised in an open woodland area. Plan on about a pound of meat per person.

Next, you'll need a spit-roasting rig. You can build one yourself—and there's no shortage of videos online to walk you through it—but we recommend renting or borrowing one. Chances are if you ask around town, someone is bound to have something you can use. Ideally you'll find a motorized spit, which will allow you to hang out with your friends more, as opposed to sitting in front of a seven-hundred-degree fire for two hours. It will be a little more expensive than the alternative, but it'll save your shoulders. The alternative is a manual spit, which is what we ended up with. If that's the case for you, just take turns with your friends. The more people you invite, the better, if only because there are more arms to turn the spit.

The Night Before the Roast

Brine your pig. Line the 50-gallon drum or cooler with a liner. Fill it about halfway with cold water and add a 2:1 mixture of salt and sugar. This is going to be a lot of salt and sugar. We suggest starting with 3 pounds of salt and 1½ pounds of sugar and going from there. You want enough in the brine that you can taste it. Because you'll be cooling the brine with ice, make it fairly strongly seasoned to accommodate the melting ice. Grab your bourbon and throw that in the mix, then add the garlic, coriander, peppercorns, and bay leaves. Add the pig, and plenty of ice, making sure the pig is submerged. Cover and allow the container to sit in a cool area overnight. Every few hours, take a look to see if you need to add more ice to keep the brine cold.

Two Hours Before the Roast

Pull the pig out of the brine and pat it dry. Using the wire, tie the pig's front legs together as tightly as possible. Repeat for the back legs. This will help protect the smaller extremities from cooking much more quickly than the thicker bits.

Once the legs are secure, affix the pig to the spit. We could try to explain how to do that here, but we guarantee that it would make things a lot more complicated than they need to be. We're guessing, though, that whoever lent you the spit will be able to give you a hand. And if not, there's always YouTube.

An Hour Before the Roast

About an hour before you're ready to begin cooking, get the fire going. First, build the base of the fire with wood stacked about a foot tall and wide enough so the flames will reach the entire length of the pig. You could also build two smaller adjacent fires to form one big fire. Let the fire burn for an hour before putting the pig on to cook so it is really ripping hot. We are not slow-roasting a pig here. This is a proper roast. We're talking about a fire that's going to get up to 700°F, but no need to stick a thermometer in the fire—if it's a giant pile of flaming wood and hot like a sweaty campfire, it's most likely the right temp.

And Now for the Roasting

Once you have a nice bed of white-hot embers to cook over, it's time to get started. It's okay if there are still a few flames; just make sure

(recipe continues)

they are about a foot lower than the pig. Situate the spitted pig over the fire. Then, using a shovel, build two mounds of ashes, one toward the head of the pig and another toward the legs. These areas take the longest to cook, so we want to have the heat closest to these.

This is when your friends will come in handy. Once the pig is going, you're in for at least a few hours of constantly rotating it—like browning, not burning a marshmallow—as well as basting it with flavorful Platza Oil (opposite).

Cook the pig until you have an internal temperature of 150°F in the shoulder (for a 40-pound pig, this will take 2½ to 3 hours), basting with Platza Oil every so often. Note that wind, rain, and snow may extend the cooking time and blow your otherwise well-timed meal out of the water. That's part of the adventure.

Once your pig is cooked, spread the mustard greens over one or two large roasting racks set in rimmed sheet trays. Set the pig on top of the greens. This will cook the mustard greens a little, as well as soak them with a pig-juice dressing. Loosely cover the whole thing with foil and let the pig rest for an hour.

Transfer the greens to a big bowl. Pour in any drippings from the pig that have collected on the sheet trays. Season to taste with salt and rice wine vinegar (if using) to balance the flavor.

At this point we could go into a long-winded diatribe about how to carve a pig, but the truth is, it's going to be confusing, and this is a total caveman meal—no one's going to care about getting a neat little slice. So don't worry about carving this up perfectly. Just start cutting and if you hit a bone, cut in a different direction. Or you can simply pull it off the bone because the meat will be so tender. Then serve the meat immediately with the mustard greens, pickles (if desired), and Fireside Fruit Chutney.

FIRESIDE FRUIT CHUTNEY

MAKES ABOUT 2 QUARTS

Pork loves fruit, especially fruit that's in season. We've included rhubarb here, but this recipe can be adapted to suit whatever you pick up at the market.

---

4 cups chopped rhubarb (from about 4 stalks) or seasonal fruit of your choice

1 cup chopped white onion

3 cups cider vinegar

3 cups packed brown sugar

1 tablespoon whole allspice

Add all the ingredients to a pot and set next to the fire, where it's hot but not blazing hot. Let the mixture cook while you're roasting your pig, until all the onions break down, the rhubarb gets sweet, and the whole mix has a loose and chunky saucelike consistency.

PLATZA OIL

MAKES ENOUGH FOR A 40-POUND PIG

While the pig was roasting—and we, too, thanks to the fire—we couldn't help but think of being in a Turkish bathhouse and being beaten by a huge hairy guy with olive branches soaked in oil. This type of massage, called *platza*, entails a beating-and-basting that's apparently for the receiver's own good. Well, same goes for that pig. Flogging the pig with flavor-soaked branches as it roasts is doing justice to that beast like any ambitious caveman gourmand would have done. Or at least we imagine.

1½ pounds (6 sticks) unsalted butter

6 shallots, thinly sliced

Salt

3 heads of garlic, cut in half along the waistline

6 bay leaves

1 tablespoon whole black and red peppercorns

1 tablespoon whole cloves

1 tablespoon coriander seeds

1 tablespoon whole allspice

1 tablespoon whole star anise

Melt the butter in the bottom of a stock pot over medium-low heat, then slowly sweat the shallots until soft and translucent, about 10 minutes, keeping the heat low enough to prevent them from browning.

Add 6 quarts of water to the pot and bring to a rolling boil over high heat. Add enough salt to make the water seawater-salty, then add the garlic, bay leaves, peppercorns, cloves, coriander seeds, allspice, and star anise.

Simmer the liquid for 30 minutes.

For applying the oil, try to find thin branches from a tree that bears edible fruit, such as an apple or peach tree. Remove the leaves and cut the whips to about 20 inches long. Bundle a manageable handful of them together, ends even to ends, and secure with wire or twine. (Or, fine, go ahead and use a long grilling basting brush.)

The trick is to constantly and completely baste the pig as it turns on the spit. This recipe makes enough to do so for about 3 hours, enough for a 40-pound pig, so adjust the batch for the size of your pig. Have your friends bring you water and stay hydrated. This task is no joke.

NOTE: COOKING LESS THAN THE WHOLE HOG
We know that you can't cook an entire pig so easily, but scaling down to a 3- to 4-pound pork loin, cooked with our meat-searing method (see page 253) would be just as rad with the greens and chutney, and especially the Turkish-Style Paella with Mussels, Currants, and Mint (page 238).

TOMATO AND SWEET CORN SALAD

SERVES 6

This is a big summer hit. It's easy to make—even easier if you get a friend on corn-shucking and string-bean-blanching duty—and the tomatoes and corn are so amazing this time of year. It's also really nice with richer, fattier dishes like roast pig, because the freshness of the salad and the acidity of the vinaigrette lighten it up.

If you can, get an assortment of tomatoes—cherries, plums, little ones, big ones, Black Princes, Speckled Romans, Green Zebras—whatever looks and tastes great. This is when going to a farmers' market is really handy because a lot of stalls will let you cut up a few and taste them. If you go to the grocery store instead, no big deal, just sniff out the most aromatic ones.

---

1 pound string beans

2 ears of fresh corn

Grapeseed or vegetable oil

Salt

3 pounds tomatoes

1 red onion, sliced paper-thin

Sherry vinegar, or red wine vinegar, or champagne vinegar (sherry vinegar will be a little bit sweeter)

Freshly ground black pepper

½ cup finely chopped fresh parsley (optional)

Bring a large pot of seawater-salty water to a boil and fill a large bowl with water and ice. Trim the stems off the beans and boil for 1 minute, just enough to set the bright green color and take a little rawness off. Drain the beans, shock in the ice water, and set aside.

Shuck the corn by peeling off its tough outer leaves and peeling off the silk sticking to the kernels. (Doing this under running water works well.) Stand each ear vertically on your cutting board and run your knife down its length, cutting where the kernels hit the cob. Collect the kernels in a bowl and set aside.

Lightly coat a large sauté pan with oil and place it on medium heat. When the oil shimmers, add the corn to the pan, season with a little salt, give a quick toss, and cook just until the kernels go from pale to bright yellow. This will remove some of the starchiness that raw corn can have and help it get a little sweeter. Remove from the heat and reserve.

Cut the tomatoes into bite-size pieces and place in a large mixing bowl. Season with salt. Mix in the onion, cooked green beans, and the corn.

Sprinkle a little bit of vinegar over the top, toss together, and taste. (The oil from the cooked corn should be enough for the salad, especially since you don't want to make this dish heavy.) Adjust the seasoning with salt and pepper, if necessary, and top with a good sprinkling of parsley (if using).

WATERMELON GRAPPA GRANITA

SERVES 6

Remember shaved ices from when you were a kid? This is just like that, only an adult version with booze.

½ cup sugar

Pinch of salt

1 cup grappa

2 pounds seedless watermelon flesh, roughly chopped

Grated zest and juice of 1 lime

WATERMELON RINDS

When you're cutting up the watermelon, save the rinds. Pickling them is an awesome way to garnish a dish, especially one that's heavy on fat. We highly recommend using our Sweet and Sour Pickle Brine (page 151) and serving them with Whole Spit-Roasted Pig with Greens (page 240).

Combine the sugar, salt, and ¼ cup water in a small saucepan and simmer until the sugar has dissolved. Remove from the heat and let cool completely, then add the grappa. The syrup must be cool; otherwise the heat will cook out the alcohol.

Add half of the watermelon to a blender or food processor and process until smooth. Pass it through a fine-mesh sieve, reserving the liquid and discarding the pulp. Blend the remaining watermelon, grappa syrup, lime zest, and lime juice until smooth. Add that mixture to the first batch. Pour into a casserole or any other shallow, freezer-safe container. Put the mixture in the freezer. Every 30 minutes, take it out and stir and scrape the mixture with a fork to break it up, until all of it has frozen. This should take about 3 hours.

Serve in glasses that have been chilled in the freezer.

TECHNIQUES
+
TERMS
+
HANDY ADVICE

TECHNIQUES AND TERMS

There's no such thing as the *best* technique. There's the best technique we know, and then there's the best technique for you. Feel free to adapt these methods to better suit you, your kitchen, and your equipment. Above all, trust yourself. You have way more cooking skills than you think you do. The intuition you use to remember to check the potatoes in your skillet is no different from the buzzer in the back of your brain that tells you the laundry's done. Plus, once you understand the "why" of doing things a certain way, the technique will follow.

Here are a few essential terms and techniques that come up frequently throughout the recipes and that are our keys to making good food. They work no matter if you're a professional chef, lifelong enthusiast, or rookie home cook.

ARROSER (ARROW-ZAY): Don't be scared of this word because it's French—it just means "to baste." In many kitchens, it means specifically to baste something with butter while it's cooking, which is how we're using it in this book. We like using this method for finishing fish and meats in the pan because it adds flavor while gently and evenly finishing the cooking process. And in the case of seafood, the foaming butter can actually help release your fish or scallops from the pan, so no more stuck-to-the-bottom, torn-up messes.

Just add a generous tablespoon or two of butter to your pan, wait a few seconds for it to melt and foam, then slightly tip the pan toward you so the butter pools.

Using a big soup spoon, continuously baste the food with the hot, foamy butter. It's a quick process, generally between 30 and 90 seconds, but you'll be amazed at the flavor it develops. It's a really luscious, gentle way to treat a piece of meat or fish after it's almost fully cooked. You can also infuse the butter with aromatics for more depth of flavor. Try throwing in a bay leaf, a smashed clove of garlic, or fresh herbs like thyme or rosemary.

We like this method so much we use it even for meats that get roasted in the oven, waiting until after the meat has rested so it's "relaxed" enough to absorb the flavor of the butter.

BLANCHING: This is just boiling vegetables quickly and then shocking them with ice-cold water to stop the cooking process. This takes the raw edge off, making them tender but still with a little "bite" or crunch. And it brightens the color of green vegetables. It's a great way to gently cook vegetables for a salad if you don't want to just serve them raw or for pre-cooking vegetables you want to char in a pan later, without worrying about burning them before cooking them through.

All that's involved is throwing together an ice bath (a fancy way of saying a big bowl filled with ice and water) and putting a large pot of water on to boil. When it comes to a rolling boil, toss in enough salt so that it tastes almost like ocean water. Add your vegetables and cook for 10 to 20 seconds before pulling one out to test for doneness. It should be softened slightly but still crisp. Once cooked to your liking, fish out the vegetables with a slotted spoon or tongs and put them directly in the ice bath.

BOUQUET GARNI, AKA AROMATICS IN A CHEESECLOTH: Sometimes when you're cooking with herbs or aromatics, you just want the flavor and not the actual bits in your food. Or you want a lot of garlic essence and don't want to eat eight cloves of garlic. That's when you make a bouquet garni—a small bundle of herbs and/or aromatics wrapped in a cheesecloth and tied with kitchen twine—so you can throw it in your dish and pull it out in one piece at the end. Letting these flavors gently infuse into your dish adds so much depth, especially to something cooked slowly like a sauce, stew, or braise.

There's no rule about what goes into a bouquet garni, but we'll give suggestions for things like thyme, bay leaf, garlic, whole black peppercorns, star anise, cloves, and so on, depending on the dish. More delicate green herbs like parsley, cilantro, chervil, tarragon, chives, and basil don't hold up quite as well under long periods of cooking. (They turn brown after about 15 seconds of heat.) These herbs add more personality and punch when added at the end to finish a dish. A good rule of thumb for figuring out which herbs are best for cooking versus those that are best added at the end is to look at their stems. Rosemary, thyme, oregano—they all have thicker, twig-like stems, and can take the heat. Compare that to the more delicate herbs listed above, which have more fragile, tender stems.

CHECKING DONENESS: Cutting into an over-cooked piece of meat or fish is not a lot of fun. But there are plenty of methods for checking doneness, so you can play with them and choose the one that you like best.

Our favorite method is using a cake tester, a thin, needlelike metal stick that's one of the most versatile tools in the kitchen. We especially like it for checking doneness because it doesn't make as big a hole as a meat thermometer, which can let a lot of the juices run out,

and it's a great way to really get to know your food. It takes some practice to get the feel for it, but we promise you'll get the hang of it.

For fish, stick the cake tester into your fillet while it's cooking. If it slides in with no resistance, it's done. But if you feel any push back, then it still needs more time in the pan.

For meat, slide the cake tester into the side of the meat you're cooking. Hold it there for 5 seconds and then put it to the underside of your bottom lip, just above your chin. Medium-rare to medium will feel slightly warm to warm. Well done will feel hot.

For vegetables, it can help check texture and tenderness. You'll know when that potato / beet / carrot / broccoli floret is done to your liking based on how easily the cake tester slides in.

For cakes. Yes, it works for them, too. After being inserted into the center of a cake, it should come out *almost* completely clean.

Or go by feel: With your left index finger, feel the mound of muscle at the base of your right thumb. That's rare. Now touch the index finger on your right hand to your right thumb and press into that muscle again. That's the equivalent of medium-rare—a little firmer, but still tender. Now clench your right fist and touch the same spot—that's what well done feels like. If you want to double-check your readings with a thermometer until you're feeling confident, insert it into the thickest part of your meat or fish and look for the following temperatures.

Fish: 125°F (medium-rare) or 135°F (medium)

Beef: 130°F (medium-rare)

Pork: 140°F (medium)

Lamb: 130°F (medium-rare)

Chicken breast: 160°F

Chicken legs: 165°F

Large game (venison, boar, etc.): 130°F

CARRYING THE SEAR: Whenever you add meat or fish to a pan with hot oil, it will displace the oil that's directly underneath it That means there's no fat between your ingredient and the pan to facilitate a nice, crispy sear. Using your hand to rotate that item 360 degrees redistributes the oil and helps create an even, flavorful crust. So when you place a steak down in a hot cast-iron skillet, for example, turn it in the pan until you know that there's oil coating both the steak and the pan where the two meet. It will cook much more evenly that way.

MEAT-SEARING METHOD: This is one great technique that you can apply to beef, chicken, pork, or lamb equally. It calls for getting a nice, crusty sear in a hot pan first, cooking it to temperature in the oven, and finishing it with butter and aromatics. With a little practice, you'll get perfectly cooked meat every time without having to memorize a bunch of different methods.

Preheat the oven to 350°F.

Heat a cast-iron pan over medium-high heat until smoking hot. Add enough grapeseed oil to generously coat the bottom of the pan. (See page 264 for why we recommend grapeseed oil over canola or vegetable oil.)

Just before searing, pat the meat dry with paper towels and season generously with kosher salt all over; it should look as though you're salting a sidewalk before a snowstorm. Add a few cracks of pepper.

Tip the pan away from you so the oil pools a bit on the opposite side and carefully place the meat in the pan to avoid splattering yourself with hot oil. Once you've set the pan down, use your hand to rotate the meat in the pan to **carry the sear** (see above), and carefully add the other pieces of meat. (If you're working with several large pieces of meat, instead of crowding the pan and causing your meat to steam, work in batches.) Keep an eye on the meat; often it will contract when it hits the heat and create a concave surface over the pan. Using a spoon or spatula, hold the center of the meat down so that it sears evenly. Once the meat is golden brown, turn it over and repeat.

Once browned on the second side, transfer the meat to a cooling rack placed over a baking sheet. If you still have meat to cook, wipe out the pan and repeat the searing process.

When all your meat is seared and resting on the cooling rack/baking sheet, place it all in the oven. Allow it to roast, flipping after a while to cook evenly. (Ideally you'd use a large spoon to do this; tongs can tear your meat, causing all the juices to run out. Of course, use your best judgment so you don't hurt yourself trying to stick your arm in a crazy hot oven or over the flames of a grill. But our vote is against tongs if you can help it.) Use a **cake tester** (see page 252) to test for doneness.

(We prefer to cook very fatty cuts of meat—like rib eye or porterhouse—a bit closer to medium than rare so that the fat actually melts. If you have a steak that is thicker than 1½ inches, drop the oven to 325°F so that the fat has a little more time to soften.)

When your meat is done, allow it to rest in

a warm place for almost half of its total cooking time.

To gently finish the meat and give it an extra dose of flavor, reheat the skillet over medium heat, add a few generous spoonfuls of butter, and **arroser** (see page 251) your fully rested meat. Allow it to rest again for another couple minutes, and serve.

FISH-SEARING METHOD: Cooking a piece of fish is a game of finesse. Whereas red meat can take really high heat and benefits from getting seared crazy hard to get a great brown crust, fish requires a more subtle touch. One of the ways we've found to pan-sear fish perfectly is by using Wondra, a kind of flour that browns at a lower temperature than regular all-purpose flour. By lightly coating your fillets just before they go in the pan, you can cook fish more gently, keeping it tender while still getting a golden, crispy crust. And because you don't have to stand vigil over a screaming hot pan, it makes the whole process a bit more mellow.

Set a pan over a medium-high flame; this is all the heat you really want for fish. Add enough oil to generously coat the bottom of the pan and let it get hot enough to look like it's dancing.

Dust the fish on both sides with Wondra, but don't season the fish with salt before cooking. Salt draws out water, and having that liquid in the pan will create steam, making it harder to get a nice, crispy crust. When the oil looks right, carefully add the fish, skin side down. You'll know if you have the right heat when the fish hits the pan: You'll hear just a bit of a sizzle as it hits the oil, just a decibel above faint. Carry the sear and then hit the fillet with a bit of salt. Go easy, though—meat can take a lot more salt than fish can, so it's okay to be conservative.

Let it ride for a bit, especially if your fillets are on the thicker side. You're looking for a golden crust to start climbing up the side of the fish. Once it hits ¼ inch, that's when you know that side is done.

Add a generous spoonful of butter to the pan. This is not only a gentle way to finish the cooking, but it also helps the fish release from the pan thanks to the steam the butter creates. So let the fish sit for a second or two as it absorbs all that foamy butter. At this point, the meat of the fish will have "opened" from all the heat, so it can really take in that flavor.

Use a big spoon or thin metal spatula to flip the fillets, taking care to not let them tear apart, and **arroser** (see page 251). How long you baste with the hot butter depends on how thick your fillets are. The easiest way to determine doneness is by using a **cake tester** (see page 252). Fish doesn't typically need a lot of time to cook, so it shouldn't need more than another 30 seconds in the pan.

Remove the fish from the pan to rest. Put it on a warm plate so it doesn't cool the fish down and let it relax for a minute before serving. Is warming a plate an extra step? Sure. But you just took the time and care to make something nice, so why not finish the job right?

GET TO KNOW HEAT: The best cooks we know have an innate understanding of heat. It's a nuanced thing and it takes practice, but tuning in to how hot something is by running with your senses instead of a thermometer will make your cooking so much better—and easier.

By sight: The viscosity or thickness of your oil says a lot about how hot your pan is. The hotter oil gets, the thinner it gets. So when your pan is smoking hot, your oil will run more easily, while at lower temperatures it will move more slowly in the pan.

By sound: There are some things in the kitchen you can't really gauge by sight or feel, particularly how hot something's cooking. But you can hear how hot your pan is by the reaction a piece of food has. For example, when we cook fish, we're listening for a soft sizzle to indicate that it's cooking at a more relaxed pace. But searing our meat at high heat should make a hard, crushing sizzle. If your more delicate ingredients sound like they're about to hit the roof, then turn down the heat. If your big T-bone is barely making a sound, turn it up.

Also, pay attention to the areas in your oven that tend to run a little hotter than others. (Don't worry, that's normal.) But understanding that, say, items in the back-left corner tend to burn a little more easily should tap into that voice in your head that says, "Check on those roasting vegetables sooner rather than later."

GREENS-WASHING METHOD: A well-dressed green salad is the easiest way to make a dish a meal, and all you really have to do is make sure the greens aren't gritty. To wash them, fill your sink or a large bowl with cold water and ice and soak the greens for about 10 minutes. Agitate the water every once in a while so that any dirt settles to the bottom. Pick the greens out of the water, repeat with fresh water, and then gently dry with a salad spinner, a clean dish towel, or a paper towel. The other thing with greens is that unless you're harvesting leafy vegetables straight from the garden, chances are they're pretty thirsty. A soak in an ice bath will crisp them up beautifully.

KNIFE CUTS, A MINI-GLOSSARY (WE DON'T REALLY CALL FOR THAT MANY DIFFERENT CUTS)

Chiffonade: Gently using the entire length of your knife to slice an item into fine shreds; often used for herbs like basil. The best way to do this is to stack several leaves, roll them up like a cigar, and slice them so that they unfurl into thin ribbons.

Dice: Creating roughly ¼-inch cubes—small but not quite minced.

Mince: Cutting an item as finely as possible without mashing it into a paste.

Rough chop: Running your knife through something once or twice—just enough so that you're getting larger pieces instead of a whole ingredient.

NUT-TOASTING METHOD: Toasting nuts really brings out their flavor and gives them a firmer, crunchier texture. Many cookbooks call for toasting nuts in a dry pan or in the oven, but to us, that's too often a recipe for charring them on one side while leaving them raw on the other, or worse, forgetting about them until they're totally burned. Our favorite method lets you control an even, golden toasting, and, well, it basically shallow-fries them in butter.

Start by melting a couple of generous spoonfuls of butter in a pan over medium-high heat. When it becomes frothy, add the nuts. Cook, stirring constantly. Once they smell faintly nutty and look golden, transfer them to a paper-towel-lined dish to drain. They will continue cooking and browning from the residual heat, so be sure to pull them off just a shade paler than you'd like.

RENDERING FAT: When you're cooking meat that has a lot of fat like duck or bacon, the key to getting it golden and crispy is to gently melt—render—that fat off. It's a simple process, but there are two things to remember. Most important, always start the meat in a cold (as in not preheated) pan, so the fat melts instead of browns. Next, you want to cook your food nice and slow over a low flame to make sure the fat dissolves evenly and doesn't burn. The best part of rendering, besides a perfectly cooked piece of meat? Straining the fat and storing in the fridge for later. Use it to fry up potatoes, cook French toast, or make a decadent piecrust.

SLICING MEAT AGAINST THE GRAIN: Meat is a little like wood. Both have grains, and both are tougher when those grains all line up. But unlike a table that you want to be strong, you want your steak or duck breast to be tender and easy to chew. So give your meat a good look. Notice how the muscle is actually made up of fibers running together. When you cut it, remember to slice across, not with, those fibers.

OTHER HANDY ADVICE

These simple philosophies are just as important as basic techniques:

THINK ABOUT COOKING "PER PERSON": This is where the "yield line" of recipes comes in handy. When a recipe says it serves four people, take a look at how much of each ingredient there is and divide it by four to get a sense of how much you're serving each guest. After a while, you'll develop a sense of how much food you like to eat or serve, and you'll be able to scale a recipe up or down perfectly for your own dinner—or put your own recipe together on the fly.

DITCH THE CLOCK: When Ithai first started cooking, he'd always ask, "How long do you cook this for?" And someone would always say, "Until it's done." It was annoying as hell, but it turns out that no two pieces of meat need to cook for exactly the same amount of time and there's no way we can tell you precisely how long something in your kitchen will take to cook. Your oven can run 10 degrees hotter than ours, your potatoes may be twice as large, or you could live at a high altitude, where water boils cooler. Plus, once someone tells you to cook something for 10 minutes, by nature you'll most likely fixate on the clock, even if the food is trying to tell you what's going on—a burning onion is a burning onion no matter how long it's been in the pan. That's why we've given descriptions of how we ideally like things to look and feel, so you can tell when it's ready.

TASTE AS YOU COOK: No two people taste things alike, which is why we say "season to taste," and it's why you should always be tasting your food throughout the cooking process, so you'll learn how the flavor is developing. (As a reminder, we'll give you cues for when you should really check.) Especially since some dishes, like soups, are better when left to cook without much salt until the end because of how the flavor intensifies as it cooks.

For the most part, when we say "to season," we're mostly talking about salt, and you'll know a dish is well seasoned when the other flavors really light up. Salt's best trick is to enhance the ingredients you're serving—not to make things "salty." Since saltiness can be subjective, feel free to get a dish to the level of seasoning you personally enjoy, then leave a nice finishing salt on the table so people can add more if they wish.

Another reason tasting as you cook is helpful is because you'll learn how different ingredients add different attributes to a dish. Think of cooking as building a complex flavor with its own structure and attitude. Think about a bowl of kale and how just that ingredient would feel in your mouth. Raw kale is delicious, but it's impossible to chew when it's dry. Once you've chopped it into thin slices and added some olive oil, it becomes richer and more pleasant to eat—but it's still pretty uninteresting. When you add something like lemon juice, not only does the acidity make it brighter, it also breaks down the kale, making it more tender. Throw in some Parmesan, and suddenly the dish has more depth and saltiness to it. Tasting a little bit at each stage helps you understand how ingredients work together as you're cooking. And, as you store all these tastes in your memory, you'll develop an instinct for knowing just what a dish needs by tasting. Tuning in to that will make you a better cook.

CLEAN AS YOU GO: It might seem funny for us to be telling you to not be a slob, but you'll become a better cook for it. When you're clean, things get easier, no matter what you're doing—you can see where everything you need is, you don't have to hunt for the next ingredient or your tools, and your brain doesn't get as frazzled. When you spill something, clean it up. If you're done with something, put it away. As you prep vegetables, throw away the discarded sections as you go.

Being organized in the kitchen allows you to be more efficient because it makes for fewer wasted movements.

Straightening as you go also makes the end of the dinner much more fun, as everyone has less cleanup to do. A perfect task for any friend who isn't cooking is to help clean your kitchen tools as you use them.

EAT AS YOU GO: There's no rule that all the food has to be cooked before people start eating. And there's definitely no rule that everyone needs to be sitting down when they dig in. If one dish is ready to go, start passing around forks. Or even better, work in a dish that's super-quick and easy like a crostini or oysters, which you can put out while the rest of the cooking is under way.

FINALLY, FAILURE *IS* AN OPTION: This book is a compilation of both our successes and our failures. That's what has allowed us to show you what we think works. We all fail, and it's a good thing. The failures are going to make you a better cook. If something doesn't come out right the first or fifth time, just roll with the punches and think about how to tackle it differently the next time. We continually retest our own recipes, even the ones we've done tons of times, because there's usually some way we can improve them. We've gotten better because of our setbacks, and so will you as long as you learn from your mistakes and refuse to give up. Just keep cooking.

TOOLS
+
PANTRY
+
SHOPPING
FOR INGREDIENTS

TOOLS

Here are our favorite tools, both essentials and things we like to have on hand if possible. You really don't need a lot of equipment to cook really nice food. (We're both used to cooking in small apartment kitchens, so we don't have space for a lot of extra stuff.)

That said, as a rule in any of life's situations, crappy tools are the worst. If you skimp, you're just going to have to replace them in a month or two. As we like to say, you can't afford to buy cheap. That doesn't mean you need to buy the most expensive equipment—more expensive does not mean better, necessarily—but do pay attention to the quality of whatever it is you're purchasing.

As you begin to assemble your small arsenal of equipment, try seeking out kitchen supply stores, if possible. Their stock might not be quite as flashy, but they'll likely carry the kind of durable workhorse gear that's built to last and is perfect for learning how to cook.

THE ESSENTIALS

KNIVES: You don't need a rack full of knives for every possible cutting scenario. We get it, it's fun, but all you really need are:

> **A chef's knife:** We recommend a Japanese knife because they are well made, last for a long time, have a finer edge than most Western knives, and hold their edge longer. Investing in a good knife will better serve your ingredients. It won't make a mush out of your herbs, produce, and meat. To find the right one for you, test-drive a friend's. Or go to a store and try out a bunch of different ones. See if they'll let you take one home and exchange it if it isn't right for you. You're looking for one that is a comfortable weight and size and basically just feels right in your hand. An 8-inch knife is perfect for most people.

> **A utility/petty knife:** This is the Japanese version of a paring knife. It is smaller than a chef's knife but still has enough length to be nice for things like chopping herbs or filleting fish.

> **A long serrated knife:** For your bread, *not* your tomatoes (as tomatoes should be sliced, not torn).

And if you're going to buy nice knives, you should take care of them. Clean them by hand after each use, and never leave them sitting in the sink. Definitely never run them through the dishwasher. Then dry them well and put them in a safe place. Also, keep them sharp.

A GOOD SET OF POTS AND PANS: You can, of course, cook on anything, but the biggest difference between a flimsy pan and good-quality one is the heat distribution; a nice, heavy-bottomed pan holds heat longer and more evenly, and it won't have hot spots that burn your food. It might be more expensive, but it's definitely worth it. Think of it this way: How many meals ruined by being scorched in a flimsy pan would it take to equal the cost of a better pan? Probably not that many, and you'll get a lot less aggravation if you're cooking in good equipment. Plus, if you take care of them by keeping them nice and clean, they'll last the rest of your life, and your children's, too. (Make sure you give both the inside and outside a good scrub after each use so grease doesn't build up.) We're big fans of All-Clad, but the same concept applies for pots and pans

as it does for knives: Try out a few and see what feels right. Here's what we like:

Cast-iron skillet: Preferably 12 to 14 inches. If you buy just one thing for your kitchen, this is a really good place to start. Invest in one that's high quality. Today you can get a decent one for about $30, but these pans aren't what they used to be. They are mass-produced and not the caliber of iron that was used years ago. They do work just fine, but a well-made, well-maintained vintage Griswold or Wagner pan is worth its weight in gold. They are not only made better; they also have a story. And if you take good care of it, you'll have it forever. We promise it will become your go-to tool, your kitchen friend. So if you can find one that's not deeply rusted or pocked on the surface, it is worth it to spend the extra $50 or so.

9-inch stainless-steel sauté pan

8-inch nonstick pan: This is perfect for eggs. They're super-cheap and easy to clean.

6-quart stock pot

CLEANING CAST IRON

There's one rule with cast iron: Never use soap to clean it. Soap removes the seasoning, the natural nonstick surface that develops over time. And it erases the "memory" of iron, the flavors that have seeped in. Instead, first pour or wipe out any extra oil or bits sticking to the bottom of the pan with a paper or cloth towel. Then use a clean, wet towel (folded up so you don't burn your hand) to wipe out the pan while it's still hot. The moisture from the towel will help steam off any oils or strong flavors left in the pan. Being careful not to burn yourself from the steam or the heat of the pan, rub the bottom and sides with the towel in circular motions until clean. Then once the pan is clean, apply a thin layer of olive oil with a paper towel to seal the pan and prevent it from rusting.

CUTTING BOARD: If you are looking to maintain a sharp edge on your knife, don't invest in a butcher block just because it's attractive, and try to avoid cutting corners by getting a cheap plastic one. Hard rubber boards like the one Sani-Tuff makes are easy to clean, don't absorb flavor or color, and don't dull your blade as much as a wooden board. Keep in mind that a great cutting board is where you and your knife will spend a lot of time.

CAKE TESTER: You'll use it for everything from checking to see that your vegetables are tender, your meat is cooked to the temperature you like it, and your fish is done. You could always use a meat thermometer instead, but the tester is efficient, cheap, and makes a smaller, less-invasive hole in what you're cooking.

MIXING BOWLS: Having a variety of sizes comes in handy for mixing and storing prepped ingredients.

SHEET TRAYS: These are perfect for roasting in the oven and also letting meat rest after it has been cooked. Getting rimmed sheet trays is preferable because they'll better contain any juices that escape from your meat.

FINE-MESH SIEVE AND/OR STRAINER: Essential when you're making stocks or straining pasta (or straining anything, really).

SPOONS: These are the extensions of your hands in the kitchen—which are truly the best

tool you have. Seriously, wash 'em and feel everything. It's how you really get to know your food. Otherwise, use a spoon to stir, taste, flip, and so on. Don't be tempted to use tongs—they just tear up your food.

SIDE TOWELS: Standard 8-inch × 16-inch dish towels work fine. Keep these handy because you can use them for just about anything—as potholders, to keep your cutting board and knives clean, to wipe your hands (you look a lot better with a clean apron), and pretty much any time you'd use a paper towel.

NICE TO HAVE

PLASTIC TAKE-OUT DELI CONTAINERS: Quart (4 cups), pint (2 cups), and half pint (1 cup). These containers work just as well as measuring cups or for figuring out portioning. Use them for storage, too.

COOLING RACKS: Ideal for letting meat rest so the juices don't pool around it, which would cause it to lose its crust as it cools.

MASON JARS: These might seem a bit trendy, but they are inarguably useful. We use them for everything from drinking a beer to mixing a vinaigrette, storing a sauce to pickling vegetables. And it's really hard to break them.

BAKING SCALE: These are very useful when baking, and they only cost about $20. Scales are much more accurate than a measuring cup. Take flour, for example. If you fill a measuring cup, there will most likely be pockets of air within the cup. So you might have the correct volume for a recipe, but you won't have the right weight. Sounds nerdy, but baking is

more science than intuition. And with a scale, you can be more certain that your baked dish will come out correctly.

OVEN THERMOMETER: So you know how hot your oven is *actually* cooking, as not all oven temperature settings are as promised. But still observe how different parts of your oven cook—most ovens don't have evenly dispersed heat.

MICROPLANE: For grating cheese and nuts and for zesting citrus.

ALUMINUM FOIL: Perfect for lining the bottom of a roasting pan or baking sheets, where oil can brown the pan instead of the food. It will cut your cleaning time in half.

KITCHEN TWINE: For trussing meat and game and tying up a bouquet garni (see page 251).

CHEESECLOTH: For combining spices in a bouquet garni (see page 251).

BLENDER OR FOOD PROCESSOR: For pureeing soups, vegetables, drinks, and lots more.

PANTRY: THE SALT AND PEPPER PHILOSOPHY

When you're using good ingredients, it doesn't take much for them to taste great. That's why you won't find much more than salt, pepper, and just a few herbs and spices (bay leaf, clove, cumin, star anise, coriander seeds) in our modest spice racks. Too often we hear people saying how they'd cook more if it meant they didn't have to buy so much stuff.

So here you go: Stop buying so much stuff. If you have a tomato in the height of its season, just hit it with some sea salt. Simple magic.

Consider these pantry basics an extension of the tools you'd buy for your kitchen:

OILS: You want to have two categories of oil on hand: the cheap stuff for cooking and the good stuff for finishing dishes and making vinaigrettes. For cooking, we usually use grapeseed oil. We recommend grapeseed oil over canola or vegetable oil because it's a good neutral-tasting oil that has by far the highest smoke point. That means that when your pan is hot enough for the oil to actually smoke, it's really damn hot. Which in turn means that your protein won't need to spend as much time in the pan to get a sear on it. And the less time your meat is getting worked in the pan, the longer it gets to relax in a nice, slow oven. Long story short: Just by using grapeseed oil, you're already getting a leg up on cooking the perfect piece of meat.

Sometimes you'll want a more flavorful oil for cooking so your food takes on that character. Higher-quality olive oils, which we use for finishing dishes and vinaigrettes, come in a variety of flavors ranging from grassy to fruity, so try a bunch and see what you like.

VINEGARS: Whether you buy red wine, white wine, champagne, balsamic, or sherry (or Jerez) vinegar is completely up to you. Depending on the flavor you're going for and how thick you want a vinaigrette, they can be fairly interchangeable. For example, a light vinaigrette is better with red wine, white wine, or champagne vinegar, whereas something more viscous and sweet would call for balsamic or sherry. As for which one you use, there's no right answer. Road-test a few to see what works for you, but definitely have some on hand to lend brightness to your food.

SALT: For cooking, all you need is kosher salt. Just pick a brand and be consistent. That's how you'll get a feel for the grains, how much you need, and how it affects the seasoning of your dish. And don't throw it in a shaker. Put it in a little bowl or a takeout container so you can grab it with your fingers. It's a lot easier to learn how salt "feels" that way and, consequently, how much you need to salt something to your preferred taste.

It's also nice to have finishing salts around. Just like you can pull a dish together with a great olive oil at the end, a good-quality sea salt adds contrast and depth. It's less about seasoning and more about adding another layer of flavor and texture, so don't depend on that last-minute pinch to save a flavorless dish.

PEPPER: Don't buy ground pepper. Buy a pepper mill and some whole peppercorns and do it yourself—the flavor will be so much more aromatic and complex.

WONDRA FLOUR: This instant flour lets you cook fish at a lower temperature while still getting the nice golden crust that comes with cooking at higher temps. It also doesn't leave that floury taste that comes with using all-purpose flour. You'll find Wondra in every good kitchen, but you can't find it in fancy markets. It's a staple of regular grocery stores because a lot of people use it to make really gnarly gravies.

SHOPPING FOR INGREDIENTS

Whether you're shopping for produce, meat, fish, cheese, charcuterie, wine, beer, or whatever else, the golden rule is "When in doubt, ask." The people who grow, butcher, or otherwise know a ton of stuff about their products are typically going to be able to shed a lot of light on the best ingredients for the job and how to prepare them.

Also, don't feel obligated to buy things at the "best" places. Even the greatest market stalls, butchers, and fishmongers have their off days. Sometimes not everything is going to look ideal. So use common sense—if something looks unappealing to you, don't buy it.

Buying Produce

Try to get to a farmers' market to buy your fruits and vegetables. There's a lot of love there. Once you get talking with the people at your favorite farm stand, and once they know you're interested in their products, they're going to tell you what's good. When we go to the market, people will see us and say, "You gotta grab this." Once, we asked the apple lady which kind she recommended for our Charred Applesauce (page 133). She said, "Let me put it this way, Honeycrisps are like Britney Spears, but these Winesaps are like *War and Peace*. Get what I'm saying?" That's someone who obviously has a relationship with what she's selling. This is why we don't automatically jump for labels like "organic" and "local." If you find people who are doing things in a way you can get behind—like carrying on the tradition of heirloom varieties and growing them without pesticides—then you'll find a good product. And when you shop at the farmers' market, you're most likely going to get things at the peak of their freshness and seasonality. Simply put, food tastes better when it's in season and taken care of.

Buying Fish

The best way to pick a cut of fish is to first take note of whether the fishmonger knows what he or she is doing. Fillets should be neat and organized, not just thrown on top of one another. If a fish market is stacking fillets, make sure the fish have been placed flesh to flesh and not skin to flesh—why would you want to bring what's on the outside to the inside? Scallops shouldn't be just thrown into a bowl and sitting in a gray pool. And nothing should ever—ever—smell fishy. Good, fresh fish should smell sweet like the ocean. (Ask to smell it before you buy anything.) The flesh should be firm and smooth in its texture (without holes) and without saw marks from shoddy butchering. A well-butchered fillet looks like the inside of an opened book—smooth and clean. If you're shopping for a whole fish, make sure the eyes are clear, not cloudy; the gills are bright red; and the body is firm, not mushy, when you press it (or ask the fishmonger to press it and show you). As with anything else you're buying, fish should be always fresh. It doesn't matter how special a fish is—if it's four days old, it's four days old. Always ask what just came in and what's good.

Buying Meat

As a general rule for all meat, don't mess around with anything that hasn't been raised right. Animals that are pent up in cages or feedlots and fed steroids and hormones and antibiotics just aren't what you want on your table or in your body. This isn't some bleeding-heart *Portlandia* stump speech, and we're not lobbying that you go out and get to know your pig's name before you have pork chops, but we are saying that these days it is pretty easy to buy meat that's responsibly raised. The integrity of the meat is better, which means it will cook better, and ultimately, it will taste better. (The same goes for eggs.)

For red meat, you're looking for healthy, tight marbling. A steak has great marbling when the white ribbons of fat run evenly through the muscle. The flesh should be firm and bright red, which means there is more blood in the tissue and that it's fresher. Gray is never a good sign, and brown is also not right. Again, look that there are no saw marks from bad butchering and instead look for smooth flesh, void of punctures. You might have high hopes about having a beef tenderloin for dinner, but if there's a big hole in it, it's not going to cook right. Be flexible and get what looks great. The same guidelines apply to pork and chicken, except pork should be a beautiful pink color and poultry a vibrant yellow or pink. When any meat has a gray quality and is giving off a lot of juice, you should buy your meat elsewhere, as this meat has most likely been frozen and maybe even improperly stored.

STORING YOUR FOOD

GREENS AND HERBS: If your grocery store is smashing their herbs or greens into plastic containers, take them out when you get home. Remove any rubber bands, too—they're strangling your produce. Wrap greens and herbs in damp paper towels and store in a covered container or drawer. That will protect them from the cold air circulating in your fridge, which will wilt them.

FRUITS AND VEGETABLES: The saying "One bad apple ruins the bunch" applies here. Plants don't like dead leaves or soggy rotten bits. Remove them. Make sure you've removed any rubber bands.

MUSHROOMS: Wrap mushrooms in wax paper and store them in a brown paper bag. They absorb flavors really easily, and the wax paper (unless like plastic wrap) keeps that out. But they still need to breathe, so you don't want to wrap them too tightly.

FISH: Store your fish flesh to flesh (as opposed to skin to flesh) on a tray lined with a paper towel (otherwise the fish will retain all the liquid, which will seep into your pan and cause steaming instead of searing) and tightly wrapped with plastic wrap. Scallops can be stored the same way, but lay them out on the tray so they're not just sitting on top of each other.

MEAT: Anything sitting in its own juices is no good. Water is the death of meat and will ultimately lead to you steaming your meat instead of searing it. Wrap each piece in butcher paper and lay them side by side on a tray, not stacked. Wrap around that a layer of plastic wrap to keep external moisture from getting in.

CHEESE: The cheese-shop-recommended way is to wrap the cheese first in parchment or butcher paper, then in plastic wrap. If you have a container or drawer that you keep all your cheese in, throw a sugar cube in there, which will absorb any moisture before the cheese does.

ACKNOWLEDGMENTS

Much love goes out to everyone who supported us through this process. In particular we'd like to give thanks to:

Rachel Holtzman, for her tireless work and dedication. There's no way we ever could have done any of this without you. We can never say it enough and are eternally grateful. Lillie O'Brian, for her wealth of sweet treats; Byron Bates, for showing everyone how much fun wine can be; Nino Cirabisi, for all the late-night drinks and dedicated support; Jerad and Justin Morrison, for giving us a better way to wake up and Annie McGee for answering our constant questions; Ash Merriman, for her fantastic food and always offering a good listen—and advice—when needed; and Jeremy and Sean Stanton, for making sure people know that meat is even more awesome when it's shown the proper love.

Our entire photo and styling team—you are some of the loveliest, most patient, hardworking bunch of ladies we've ever had the pleasure of working with. Nicole Franzen, you have an incredible eye for photographic food; Chelsea Zimmer, you made our food look as beautiful as we ever could have imagined; and Kaitlyn DuRoss, your eye for piecing together the perfect moment and scene will no doubt make folks want to eat our food. To Milk NY Equipment, thank you for your incredible generosity and helpfulness.

Anna Sheffield, for bringing a bit of the New Mexico magic; Bob and Cora Hales, for sharing their home; Janis Donnaud, for always having our backs and being a fantastic agent; Doris Cooper and Francis Lam, for helping us bring our ideas to life and making the journey that much more enjoyable; Lisa Callaghan, for giving us a better experience in the kitchen; James Lowe, for being both a patient and brilliant teacher; Geordy Pearson, for always being there and being gracious; Ben Freemole and John McCarthy, for being patient teachers and true friends; Justine Kahn, for her endless support and steady direction down a winding road; Maria Pi-Sunyer de Gispert, for her patience, love, and positivity throughout.

Our families, for being our bedrock.

A SHORT LIST OF PEOPLE, PLACES, AND THINGS WE LOVE

ALL-CLAD METALCRAFTERS
all-clad.com

BONFIGLIO & BREAD
748 Warren Street
Hudson, NY 12534

CLAM LAB CERAMICS
Claire Catillaz
clamlab.com

THE CRIMSON SPARROW
746 Warren Street
Hudson, NY 12534

HUDSON WINE MERCHANTS
341 Warren Street
Hudson, NY 12534

KORIN KNIVES
57 Warren Street
New York, NY 10007

LENNY BEE PRODUCTIONS
403 Wittenberg Road
Bearsville, NY 12409

THE LOBSTER PLACE
Chelsea Market
75 9th Avenue
New York, NY 10011

THE MEAT HOOK
100 Frost Street
Brooklyn, NY 11211

THE MEAT MARKET
389 Stockbridge Road
Great Barrington, MA 01230

MONTGOMERY PLACE ORCHARDS
8 Davis Way
Red Hook, NY 12504

NORTH PLAIN FARM
P.O. Box 61
Great Barrington MA, 01230

OTTO'S MARKET
215 Main Street
Germantown, NY 12526

SIGHTGLASS COFFEE
270 7th Street
San Francisco, CA 94103

SUNRISE MARKET
4 Stuyvesant Street, 2nd Floor
New York, NY 10003

INDEX